Path of the Kabbalah

Path of the Kabbalah

by David Sheinkin, M.D.

Edited by Edward Hoffman, Ph.D.

PARAGON HOUSE
NEW YORK, NEW YORK

Published by Paragon House, Inc.
2 Hammarskjold Plaza
New York, N.Y. 10017

Library of Congress Cataloging-in-Publication Data

Sheinken, David, M.D.
    Path of the kabbalah.

    1. Caballa   I. Title.
BM526.554   1986   296.1'6   86-18686

ISBN 0-913757-69-1

Editor's Preface

Though I never met David Sheinkin, I feel that we have touched, in a way. For in the memories of those who knew him well—family members, friends, colleagues, and students—clearly he continues to be a source of spiritual direction and inspiration. Through their warm, personal reminiscences and my hours spent editing the hundreds of transcribed pages of his lectures on Jewish mysticism, something of Dr. Sheinkin's light has come to shine through for me. I wish to offer special thanks to all at the David Sheinkin Memorial Fellowship in this regard. It is my hope that this book will become a valuable part of David Sheinkin's legacy—and help elevate many with his illuminating teachings.

Edward Hoffman, Ph.D.

To David's first and finest teachers,
Sam and Hannah Sheinkin.

Foreword

My husband David was truly a wandering Jew, his life a quest for truth and meaning. He refused to accept the bondage of teachers or teachings that said—This is your truth—go no further. As a result, he was always questioning, exploring, discovering and growing. His search ultimately brought him home to a body of knowledge rooted in his heritage—the Kabbalah.

The last years of his life were dedicated to the study of Jewish mystical teachings. David felt deeply fortunate to have Rabbi Arieh Kaplan as his friend and guide through this labor of love.

My husband's work and his self-realization were one in the same. Whether learning or teaching, he was shaping himself, reaching for the meaning of his being. In that process, he also inevitably illuminated the path for others. A deep inner sense of unity between the temporal and the eternal served as his guide, and so whether functioning as a father, a husband, a physician, a teacher or a student, he held an awareness that this moment was his life's work.

And so this book too is his life's work. I can see after reading this manuscript, that David, even beyond his own lifespan, continues to teach us and vitalize our learning with his own.

I am enormously grateful to Ed Hoffman and to the David Sheinkin Memorial Fellowship for giving voice to David's spiritual quest.

Lynn Sheinkin

Contents

CHAPTER ONE

The Kabbalistic Path

CHOOSING A SPIRITUAL PATH

Before we examine some of the specific aspects of Jewish mysticism, it is important for us to understand accurately some basic notions about spirituality in general. By this I mean that we are more than just body and mind; we have a spiritual part to ourselves. This can be a poetically appealing or comforting idea to people, but my goal in explicating this material is to help make that idea real and tangible. Through the Kabbalah, I hope to enable the spiritual part of us to actually come alive. Indeed, it should become as much an obvious part of us as the hand that we see and feel when we awaken. The Kabbalah represents one of the many paths that have existed throughout history to accomplish this.

It is also important to emphasize that each of us needs to find the one spiritual path that is right and to follow it closely. From my own professional vantage point as a psychiatrist, many analogies come to mind. For example, there are a variety of different schools of psychology and psychotherapy. Each school's adherents argue forcefully that it embraces the correct approach to the human mind and that the others are wrong or incomplete. Yet, clearly, some people are helped by a particular school and some are not. I think this suggests that there are probably many different ways to help someone with psychological problems and that success of any given approach depends largely on the therapist—his or her knowledge of that approach and the "match" with a particular client. That is, it does not seem very likely that there is only one valid method of psychotherapy that works equally well for all. People are obviously complex and we all differ in various ways from one another.

The same seems to apply in the field of nutrition. In fact, this realm may be a closer analogy to that of the spiritual because there are as yet no formal nutritional schools where one can learn direct, clinical applications as one can for psychotherapy. In other words, suppose a physician today wants to practice nutritional counseling; no formal schools really exist to provide that kind of specialized training; the learning must for the most part be done on one's own. Hopefully, this situation will begin to change. But as a physician, having decided some time ago to learn the intricacies of nutrition, I came to a very interesting observation—one relevant to the spiritual realm as well.

When I first explored the nutritional field, I found that many so-called experts existed—each with his or her fiefdom, disciples, and detailed teachings for health and well-being. Furthermore, I found that I could place together perhaps a dozen of the leading books in the field, examine their respective recommendations, and find obvious contradictions among them. For instance, if one closely adheres to what each of the nutritional authorities tells him to avoid eating, he will discover that there is absolutely nothing left to eat, because there is not one food that at least one of them does not consider harmful. Conversely, looking at what each authority will allow one to eat, if he chooses carefully, at least one expert will be found who will permit a certain food; and thereby he can consume just about anything.

The moral of this is that if the seeker has enough books, he can develop any system he likes simply by picking and choosing among the different sources. By adhering to what one expert tells him to follow and what another expert tells him to avoid, he can create his own program. In reality, though, such a program would most likely consist of exactly what the seeker is doing right now: it would be little more than a rationalization for his current values and behaviors.

Given, then, that we can find an authority who will support virtually anything, the logical question becomes: what will really lead to health? How can all these experts give seemingly contradictory advice and still attract so many exponents who swear by their particular methods? My conviction is that it is indeed possible for all of these authorities to be right. There is more than one path of well-being, but the key is that each path must be whole unto itself and must be followed in its entirety. If a person follows any of the major nutritional paths in this way, the chances are that he or she will experience good results.

In other words, each nutritional path has a certain inherent logic. It allows certain foods and behaviors because these are counter-balanced by other foods and behaviors: a balance exists within the system. There are many ways that a balance can be created, but each system sets up that harmony for the individual who adheres to it. However, once the person starts to pick and choose among the various nutritional systems, he or she violates the inner integrity of whichever system is being examined. And that is a sure means to negate the benefits available to the seeker.

The same principle exists for the spiritual dimension in our lives. Many different spiritual systems have been promulgated and practiced throughout world history. Some have existed for thousands of years and have stood the test of time as well as anything that we know of. Some of humanity's greatest figures have been involved with such systems, have lived them, and have taught them. It is possible to choose any one of these paths and, irrespective of which one is picked, to arrive at the same destination.

The spiritual paths are different from one another, but each path has an internal consistency. Today, unfortunately in a way, the very accessibility of information about all these spiritual traditions has created some real problems for people. Such problems would have been almost unthinkable just a few generations ago. We can look over the various spiritual systems and say: this idea I really like, but that one I don't; this ritual or practice seems very uplifting to me, but that one seems boring and irrelevant. With so much information available to us, it is easy to conclude: I'll pick this idea from this tradition, that idea from that one, and several of those rituals and practices from a third. One can quite methodically adopt the concepts and methods that appear the most sensible or beneficial, thinking that he or she is thereby engaged on a path that will lead to true spiritual growth. But will it? I don't think so.

As our analogy to the nutritional field suggests, each spiritual tradition has an internal consistency. Certain aspects within the system are offset or counter-balanced by other aspects within the same system. If one does not follow the system in its entirety, one loses the whole inner harmony that it seeks to establish. This is why people can spend literally years drifting from one time-honored spiritual system to another without gaining significant benefits. The problem is not that the systems don't work anymore or that there is something "wrong" with the individual; the problem is that by picking and choosing from among various systems, the person has missed the balance that each system offers in its entirety.

This crucial idea applies to many aspects of life. In the holistic health group with which I am affiliated, a person may be given a diet to follow. However, the diet is generally not given in isolation: it is given together with a specific exercise program and other daily regimens conducive to health. Our goal is to balance what the person needs; we may change the diet to enhance or offset the effects of a certain necessary exercise program. Thus, for an individual to tell us, "I like the exercise regimen but I don't think I will change my diet just now," may be very foolish and even harmful. The person who adopts this attitude is ultimately short-changing himself or herself, because the balancing effects of our system are ignored.

Another interesting application of this principle can be seen in the martial arts schools now flourishing around the United States. Because of the fear and tension in our society, many people are flocking to martial arts schools to learn how to defend themselves in the event of violent crime. There are literally thousands of places now to learn Kung-Fu or Karate or other Oriental systems. Within a relatively short period of time, one can acquire a black belt or learn various techniques of physical combat. One may even become able to inflict bodily damage on a would-be attacker. But is this what the martial arts traditions are really about?

Historically, these Oriental systems are worlds apart from the prevalent situation in the United States today. Tai-Chi, for example, was never taught as a storefront operation designed to teach methods of physical combat. In olden times, one would essentially enroll in an institution, usually a religious temple, where he would go and live for many years. His training would embrace many aspects of life. He would be placed on a special diet; he would be required to learn various forms of meditation. Much of his day would be spent in learning the rigors of self-discipline in a monastic way; from his first waking moments to his last conscious thoughts at night, his life would be carefully regulated and supervised in a religious atmosphere.

Central to such a way of life would be transmitted teaching. Part of that teaching would encompass the realm of the body—and of the martial art. He would certainly learn the details of the martial art, so that he would become skilled in physical combat; however, such fighting techniques would be taught as only a small part of an overall philosophical, ethical, and spiritual body of knowledge.

For example, Tai-Chi teaches that one should never use the martial art to hurt another until he has demonstrated successfully to his masters that he can perform healing. Adepts stress that the same energy used destructively in physical combat can be used positively in healing. They also emphasize that the individual is responsible for every hurt he inflicts during combat, so that he must know how to heal the person he has just injured.

Imagine, then, the tremendous difference between this ancient system as traditionally practiced and the storefront enterprises today of our own society. In the past, a person interested in learning Tai-Chi would be expected first to master many other, related aspects, including the ability to heal others. Years would be spent in rigorous training in ethics, philosophy, and spirituality; the initiate would be taught how to avoid fighting and how to take responsibility when fighting was necessary. Clearly, our own culture—for reasons partly related to fear of crime—has taken certain ideas and methods out of their original context.

Now, the kind of person who graduates from a storefront martial arts operation is going to be very different from the one who has taken the training in its entirety. He will certainly lack the inner balance of his better trained counterpart. The same principle applies to the spiritual realm. Thus, for example, it is not uncommon for people to say, "I understand that this spiritual system teaches meditations for healing purposes. I'd like to learn those." Or, "I have a problem with my digestion. What meditation can I learn to heal that?" Such a person expects that the meditation will work like a pill because that is how our dominant medical model works. We go to a doctor, tell him that we have a headache, and he is supposed to prescribe a pill to make it go away. Or, we have a complaint about liver pains, and he is supposed to prescribe a medicine to cure that problem.

In this sense, the medical model has discouraged many people from persevering in a particular spiritual system; spiritual teachers are not like doctors prescribing pills for their patients' complaints. Indeed, the opposite is usually the case. An individual may approach a spiritual teacher and say, "I want to learn such and such..." And, typically, the teacher replies, "Fine, but in order to do that you must first..." and proceeds to describe years of disciplined activity. All the individual wanted was to learn an apparently simple technique or practice, and the teacher seems to be speaking about an entire apprenticeship.

It is traditional, in fact, for the would-be martial arts practitioner to be initially sent away by his prospective teacher. In the East, an individual might be rebuffed several times before being accepted as a true student; this might be a form of testing the person's desire to learn. Or, the would-be student might be given a seemingly very mundane task to perform, such as cleaning the building or practicing a single bodily position for months and months. The teacher might say, "Practice this position for three years and then we will proceed." And the seeker would be expected to do just that. How many of us today possess the discipline, patience, or even the mind-set to behave in this way?

It is easy to be misled today into believing that spirituality merely involves learning certain techniques. For millennia, Kabbalists have viewed their path as embracing an entire way of life. On this point, the present-day spiritual teacher Patricia Sun relates an interesting story that goes as follows.

> There was once a village that was burdened with a great problem. Its inhabitants sought out a great sage and asked for his help. Not being quite sure what to do, the sage answered, 'Well, I need some time to think about this.' Then he went off into the nearby woods to meditate; because he was hungry, he brought an avocado with him to eat. He found a rock and began to meditate upon the villagers' problem.
>
> While meditating, the sage suddenly had a revelatory experience. A celestial light appeared before him and he felt infused with divine knowledge. The sage now possessed the complete solution to the villagers' great difficulty. He returned from the woods to them and announced, 'I have the answer for you. Let me tell you what happened. I took an avocado and I went out into the woods. Then I sat down on a rock and I began to meditate. All of a sudden, a celestial light appeared.'
>
> Thereupon, the villagers all asked him at once, 'Which rock was it? What kind of avocado were you eating?' To this day, the villagers are still arguing over which rock the sage sat on and what type of avocado he had been eating.

In this same way, we can be so caught up in the specific process of spiritual development that we lose sight of the whole objective. It is our whole way of life that matters in this realm.

WHICH SPIRITUAL PATH TO TAKE?

Based on these considerations, the question then becomes: if there are so many spiritual paths, which one should I take? How can I know which way to adopt? How can I know which one is better? Perhaps, we should begin this topic with the notion that there are many spiritual traditions that are equally good and that the issue of "better or worse" does not necessarily apply. In fact, before one decides on a particular system it might be good to explore several of them.

In this context, I am not opposed to a certain amount of seeking across various traditions. Such experimentation can reassure us that we are not missing out on any spiritual path, and satisfies our curiosity about the many paths that exist. But what criteria should guide us when we evaluate spiritual traditions? One consideration is to find a path that lies close to our own roots or which has developed close to our own origins. In this context, it is helpful to realize that both Western and Eastern spiritual traditions have existed for thousands of years. Not surprisingly, these traditions have shown marked differences for centuries. The Eastern paths have evolved from a completely different way of life, a completely different set of cultures, and a completely different array of time rhythms, value systems, and worldviews. Those of us who live in the West may therefore find more suitable a spiritual path that is consistent with our own way of life.

Why is this? Because there is simply no way to adopt an Eastern path and live successfully in an environment like New York City or Los Angeles. One can say that he or she will meditate, perform most of the rituals and practices, and maintain the expected outlook. But remember our earlier point: once we start picking and choosing which features to follow, we have lost the whole inner balance and harmony of the system. The issue is not that the Eastern paths are inferior to the Western ones, but that in our society the Eastern paths are doomed to be imbalanced whereas the Western ones at least offer the possibility for wholeness.

Within the Western world, several different spiritual traditions have flourished. Yet, they all share certain commonalities that make them pertinent for Western people. Also, within each spiritual tradition, an exoteric and a more or less separate esoteric path can be identified. For instance, the Catholic Church, the Greek Orthodox Church, and the Jewish religion all have well-defined and well-established paths, as well as secret paths historically known to only a very few.

The Kabbalah represents the secret, mystical part of Judaism. My purpose in focusing on the Kabbalah is not to persuade the spiritual seeker to adopt this path; nor is it to convert him or her to Judaism. Rather, it is only to convey an overview of the Kabbalistic path so that the seeker can understand it much the way one might look at any culture or religious tradition. For example, one might be interested in studying American Indian folklore or mythology or mysticism; that does not necessarily mean that he or she is going to join an American Indian tribe. Nonetheless, one's life may be greatly enriched by such study.

Also, exploration of the Kabbalah can be of help regardless of what spiritual path the seeker decides to stay with. The Kabbalistic path is the basis for all the later Western paths; all are in some sense derivatives of it. How and why that happened historically we will examine later in this book.

The Jewish Mystical Tradition

In examining the Kabbalah, we must begin with certain basic concepts. Through these, we can understand what the Kabbalah teaches, its fundamental assumptions and tenets. Our approach is not that we must necessarily "believe" the Kabbalistic worldview, but that we have to adopt it for purposes of comprehending the principles of Jewish mysticism. Think of American Indian spirituality: to understand the Indian's outlook in praying to a deer before he hunts and kills it, one must set aside one's own value system and say, "Well, I will look at it as if it were true." By accepting the "as if" attitude, one can obtain a much clearer picture of what the American Indian is trying to do.

First, what does the word "Kabbalah" mean? Its literal meaning is "to receive". This leads us to the first of several fundamental aspects of Jewish mystical thought; for all of these, we must adopt an "as if" attitude to gain fully from our exploration.

The question of what we receive in the Kabbalah brings us to the ancient Jewish conception of the Torah: that there was a divine communication. In some moment of history, God communicated with man and through this communication a set of laws, a book, was written. This, of course, is the communication between God and Moses. God communicates to Moses and instructs Moses to write down certain things, and Moses does so. According to Jewish tradition, Moses was merely the scribe for this communication. He functioned very much like a modern secretary taking dictation, only the dictation was coming directly from God. This is how the "Five Books of Moses" came into being.

Now, in the process of this heavenly transcription, certain details needed to be explained. God may have said to Moses, "Write down such and such," and then explained something to Moses as to what had just been dictated. In this way, the completed process established a body of knowledge that was written down and a body of knowledge that existed orally, as God's original oral communication to Moses. This oral communication related directly to the written material.

In Judaism, therefore, there are really two Bibles. Without this awareness, one would become lost in the orchard of the Kabbalah very quickly. The two Bibles are the written Bible and the oral Bible. The oral Bible is a commentary on the written Bible. Perhaps it would be analogous to a college class where the professor lectures on a novel the students are reading; the lectures are a commentary and reflection of the novel, not the novel itself.

Another example of this principle might involve the learning of technical information. Suppose you want to learn a specific skill, such as carpentry or tailoring. Such skills are not really described in books, yet people have been performing these for centuries according to certain rules. Some of the information could be recorded in books, but much is by necessity transmitted orally.

Our second point is that the oral Bible itself consisted of two distinct aspects. There was a part that was taught to everyone; and there was a hidden, secret part, taught only to certain select individuals. And so, there is a written Bible and an oral Bible which itself is subdivided into common knowledge and very secret knowledge. Why the secret knowledge? This question leads us to another fundamental Kabbalistic principle: that the Bible or Torah represents, in modern terminology, "an owner's manual to the universe".

THE SECRET BIBLE

Modern science and technology give us a very clear analogy for the secret part of the Bible. Think of the Bible as an owner's manual, whose purpose is akin to the manual that comes with any appliance or high-tech item that one purchases. The owner's manual tells how to use the appliance. All of us have had experience with such booklets; some are very small and some are very thick. As a pilot, I know that the manual I have for my airplane is very thick, with considerable information in it. In fact, it is a whole book. But it does not teach me how to fly an airplane by any means, nor how to read a map or what to do in various situations. Rather, the manual tells me only how to operate the specific machinery in the plane.

For instance, if I want to turn on the radio, the manual tells me, "this button turns the radio on", or "this knob changes the frequency"; but it doesn't tell me the radio's purpose. That I have to know myself. Nor does the manual relate what frequency to tune into—for that information there are other booklets. In other words, the owner's manual tells me how to operate every piece of equipment on the airplane, but that is all. Similarly, an owner's manual for a refrigerator will not tell how to build a refrigerator or how to fix it, but merely how to operate it: how to plug it in, maintain it, get the ice out, and related matters.

In an analogous way, the Bible can be seen as an owner's manual to the cosmos. Kabbalists have taught for centuries that when humans were given the planet, they were also given an owner's manual that tells us how to operate the planet. Yet Kabbalists regard this manual, the Bible, as more than merely a guidebook as to what we must do on the planet. They believe the Bible is actually telling us something about the circuitry of the universe—how it is "wired"—so that, in theory at least, a knowledgeable individual could learn how to manipulate the very forces of Creation.

It is for this reason that the leaders of the Jewish people have historically been very concerned about making this information too accessible to the world. What happens if we give very powerful tools to those who lack the training to use them? Certainly we would not give sticks of dynamite to young children to play with. That would be very foolish. At the same time, though, to ban dynamite altogether would not make much sense, for dynamite can be very constructive, helping to build bridges and roads.

Jewish spiritual leaders have therefore always sought to place some measure of control over who has access to the secret oral tradition. Just as dynamite can be very dangerous to the unskilled, so too is the Kabbalah regarded. And just as dynamite can be destructive in the hands of unprincipled or criminal people, so too can the knowledge embodied in this ancient system. The Jewish sages have consequently been very careful to restrict the Kabbalah to those with the proper training and attitude.

How do we restrict information, though? One method is to not write it down. Such a step immediately limits access; this was a chief reason why there was an oral rather than a written component to the Bible. Another reason for the existence of the oral tradition has little to do with motives of safeguarding material: it relates to the simple fact that much that we want to know about the world can only be learned orally. In learning any real craft, for example, most of the training has to be oral in nature. For these two reasons, then, Judaism has incorporated an oral tradition alongside—and complementary with—the written tradition of the Bible.

Moses, therefore, was in a position to select carefully— literally, to hand-pick—the people whom he was going to entrust with this third portion of the Bible. All Jews had access to the written Bible; and they had access to the first part of the oral Bible, too. But only a highly select group was thus given access to the third portion, the most esoteric. From generation to generation, that select group transmitted this secret, oral information. The Jews' spiritual leaders believed that this process would last forever, but it did not. It lasted a very long time—some fifteen hundred years—but eventually much of this third portion of the Bible was indeed written down.

JUDAISM AND EARLY CHRISTIANITY

The question often arises as to the relation of the Kabbalah to Christianity as well as to post-Temple Judaism. Certainly there have been "Christian Kabbalists" in the West for many centuries. An historical overview of early Christianity, especially in the context of mystical thought, may be helpful in our understanding of Kabbalistic teaching. We all know, of course, that Christianity began within Judaism. Jesus was certainly a Jew. All of the twelve apostles were Jews as well, as were all of the early Christians. For a long time one could be a Christian and a Jew at the same time and for many years the issue of being Christian *or* Jew was not an important one. It definitely became a problem, however, as the decades after Jesus' death elapsed.

According to the available evidence today, the early followers of Jesus numbered between one hundred and two hundred. These were his "core" of personal followers during his last years and these people were all Jews. After his death, most of those who became Christian were also Jews and they comprised two distinct groups. The first were those people who were of Jewish ancestry and practiced the Jewish tradition. The second group were those who were not Jewish by ancestry but who lived in the Land of Israel and by circumstance therefore adopted most of the traditions of Judaism. This second group were known as the *proselytes*, and many of these individuals converted to Christianity or began to believe in its tenets. Immediately after Jesus' death, Christianity was simply a sect within Judaism.

Historically, this was a time when the Romans controlled most of the known world and certainly the area of Judea and the Temple site. At that time it was quite a privilege to be a Roman citizen and it was difficult to become one without having been born into this status—one would often have to pay a considerable amount of money for the privilege. However, some of the Roman emperors did grant Roman citizenship to people within their empire, depending on certain conditions such as where they lived.

Paul, who became Saint Paul, was a Roman citizen and a Jew at the same time. He was granted Roman citizenship by virtue of the area in which he was born. Paul was against those Jews who were following Jesus. At one point he decided to journey to Damascus, round up these followers, bring them back and have them persecuted. On the way to Damascus, he became blind and then had a vision in which Jesus appeared to him. Jesus asked Paul, "Why are you persecuting me?" And, thus, Paul became a believer in Jesus. He had himself baptized, and with his baptism, his blindness disappeared. Paul began to preach that Jesus was actually the Messiah.

Apparently, though, Paul possessed an abrasive personality that upset people. He agitated many of Jesus' own followers because of his harshness and agitated many opposed to Jesus' followers as well. Eventually Paul went off to live by himself in the desert for a number of years to pursue spiritual enlightenment. Later he returned to active service and tried to recruit as many people as possible to accept Jesus as the Messiah. To do this, he began to accept anyone—not just Jews or proselytes —into the Christian fold, so long as he or she were willing to regard Jesus as the Messiah.

It was a true turning point in the history of Christianity and Judaism. Essentially before this historical moment, all those following Jesus were Jews and observers of Mosaic Law. Paul shifted the Christian stance to state: The crucial thing is to believe in the divinity of Jesus, even if you don't follow all of the biblical law. We'll accept you and I'll baptize you, and you will be a Christian.

Paul's stance was opposed by many of the Christians of the day: those who followed Mosaic Law and did not want to dilute their Judaism by bringing in people who rejected Judaism as a whole. Thus the first rift within the Jewish sect of Christianity was formed: between Paul's followers, who accepted everyone, and Peter's followers, who sought to remain faithful to Mosaic Law. Both Paul and Peter were arrested and later executed by Roman authorities. Peter was crucified at the Vatican and that is why the Vatican is called Saint Peter's. As a Roman citizen, Paul was given the more "merciful" execution of beheading. As time progressed, though, the rift that had begun with these two leaders became more and more significant. Another key factor historically was the Roman policy toward the religions of the countries they occupied. The Romans typically forbade the practice of new religions, but tolerated the observance and practice of existing ones. This policy was very important to the early Christians because they could successfully argue that they were practicing only a form of Judaism, that they were really Jews and not establishing a new religion. But this security in being Jewish was not permanent either. During the reign of Herod (37 B.C.-4 A.D.), the Jews had revolted against Rome. Led by fanatics known as the Zealots, they decided to end all Roman domination over the Holy Land and the Temple. Until this point the Roman leaders had been fairly tolerant of the Jews, but this bitterly-fought revolt changed that drastically. Suddenly it was no longer politically safe to be affiliated with Judaism.

The Christians began to realize that they were now putting themselves in jeopardy by continuing to call themselves Jews. Throughout the Roman empire many Christian leaders were executed by the government. By being associated with Judaism, the Christians ran great political risks; but to declare themselves harbingers of a new religion was just as dangerous. In this perilous situation, Christian leaders decided to preserve Jesus' teachings which previously had been orally transmitted. Thus, sometime between sixty-five to one hundred years after Jesus' death, the New Testament, as we have it today, was written.

It is important to remember that Jesus never wrote anything in terms of a text; his teachings were all oral. As is true for Judaism, there was undoubtedly an oral part to his teachings meant for all and a more secret part—a kind of Christian Kabbalah—which was reserved for a select few. Was Jesus a Kabbalist? His teachings suggest that he was a Kabbalistic adept and that much of his message was rooted in the Kabbalah.

Jesus probably attracted many of his followers because he preached publicly about matters that the Jewish leaders were not disseminating. As to whether Jesus was actually the

Messiah, it is interesting to note that Catholic theologians today are fiercely debating the issue of whether Jesus really proclaimed himself the Messiah. Some argue that Jesus never issued such a claim and that it was only made about him. Clearly some of Jesus' followers indeed regarded him as the Messiah whereas others did not; though initially all of them were Jews and observers of Mosaic Law.

Under massive Roman persecution, Christianity became an underground religion and grew rapidly in this form. In 327 A.D., Emperor Constantine accepted Christianity as the official religion of Rome. The religion could now come out into the open, but by then a great deal of animosity between Jews and Christians had developed. One reason for this must be attributed to the decision of the rabbis of the day. By the end of the second century A.D., more and more people were being converted to Christianity. Paul's own proselytizing efforts had been phenomenally successful: he traveled from place to place, and converted many people from pagan religions to Christianity, not simply practicing Jews or those who emulated Jewish observance. Because Christianity still seemed to be a Jewish sect, such conversion began to loom as a danger to the integrity of Judaism as a separate religion.

The rabbis grew increasingly worried that all of Judaism would become dissipated through the cursory involvement of tens of thousands of new converts to Christianity. Historically, Judaism had made conversion very, very difficult and now Paul and his followers were making it as easy as possible. Therefore, the rabbis made a decision with tremendous implications: they decreed that henceforth one could be a Jew only if the Mosaic Law was followed to the letter. They forced the many "Jewish Christians" to choose either Judaism or Christianity. One could no longer be both at the same time.

The rabbis' decision did not sit well with the many Christians who still wished to think of themselves as Jews. As a result, a counter-move occurred. In such texts as the Gospel of Saint John and the Book of Revelations, Christian leaders began to condemn Judaism as dogmatically blind to the new truth of the Lord. They began to denounce the Jews as having failed to see the Light and as obstinately refusing to embrace the New Covenant between man and God. This outlook can be seen as the historical foundation for the centuries of anti-semitism which have followed.

To retaliate against Jewish rejection of Christianity, Christian leaders began to institute a whole series of tenets to show their separation from Judaism. They transformed many of the Jewish fast days into days of feasting. They took the concept of the Sabbath Day—basic to Judaism—and changed it from Saturday to Sunday. They declared as obsolete all the dietary laws found in the Bible. By doing this, Christian leaders could put prospective converts to the test: if they really believed in Jesus and wanted to join the Christian community, they could no longer observe Mosaic Law. They had to deliberately violate what Judaism considered holy.

By the time Emperor Constantine accepted Christianity, many generations of antagonism between Christians and Jews had elapsed. The rift between the two groups had become solidified and not easily undone. Ironically, there is no question that Jesus observed Mosaic Law his whole life; nor is there any question that the disciples did so as well. The real rift began centuries after their deaths. Before that, Christians were essentially Jews and able to participate in Judaism as others did.

JEWISH HISTORY: A KABBALISTIC VIEW

From the Kabbalistic perspective, there was a thousand-year period of Jewish history during which divine prophecy existed. This prophecy was very much linked to the Ten Commandments—their physical presence on two tablets of stone kept in a special ark in a special area in the Temple. Later in the book we will examine this topic in considerable detail. Suffice it to say here that when the Ten Commandments were kept in their proper place, they acted analogously to a radio transmitter to allow celestial communication to occur. Just as a radio must be plugged into a live circuit, the Ten Commandments, when properly placed in the Temple, allowed prophecy to be transmitted from the transcendent world to ours.

Those who foresaw the destruction of the First Temple took the ark and hid it in a labyrinth built deep under the Temple. The purpose of this labyrinth was to safeguard the safeguard the holy ark and seal it off should the Temple ever be destroyed. According to Jewish history, the ark was carried down and sealed off. The entrance to the maze was likewise sealed, for the fear had long existed that such a powerful transmitting device could cause unimaginable devastation if it fell into the wrong hands.

When the Temple was destroyed, then, the ark was never found because it had already been hidden. But at the same time, the prophets who were still living understood that communication between God and man would now be different. They would not lose their prophetic gifts, but those after them would no longer be able to achieve the same level of prophecy. In the end there were three major prophets left and they all died within one month of one another. This was precisely a thousand years after Moses' original prophecy, so it was a thousand years that divine prophecy lasted. They knew, through divine prophecy, that with their deaths prophecy would cease and humanity would enter this stage that it has been in ever since.

Kabbalists believe that for this reason some of the secret, oral tradition was written down, for the prophets had to afford some access to it after their deaths. In those years before and just after the Temple's destruction, the prophet was always available to provide divine guidance to people. If an individual were unable to understand the secret code of the Bible, the prophet could enter into a trance state and obtain the celestial information. That way men and women had a channel to the Holy One—almost like a heavenly radio transmitter. But with the imminent ending of prophecy, the prophets were concerned about the future spirituality of the Jewish nation. They knew that other spiritual paths existed and they did not wish the Jews to abandon their own.

The prophets' solution, therefore, was to attempt the establishment of a superstructure of laws and regulations intended to keep the Jewish people from straying from the Jewish path. To a certain extent, the prophets succeeded; to a large extent, they failed, for today many Jews have gone off to other paths.

Jewish tradition teaches that Moses himself wrote the

Bible from divine "dictation". Interestingly, we are told that he wrote not one Bible but thirteen copies of it. He kept one with the holy ark and then a separate copy was given to each of the twelve tribes; from these scrolls, other copies were made. All the subsequent copies, including those used in synagogues today, must be handwritten in precisely the same way that Moses wrote them; these rules have been followed for millennia in Judaism.

This topic brings us to an intriguing historical account as to how the Hebrew Bible was first translated. According to Jewish tradition, there was an emperor who wanted the Hebrew Bible translated into Greek. He summoned seventy of the greatest Jewish scholars of the time and ordered them to develop a Greek translation of the Hebrew Bible, written out in the traditional manner.

The scholars were now in a quandary because they had to follow the emperor's dictates or be killed. However, they did not wish to turn over to him what they regarded as a handbook to the universe. Of course, they knew that without the secret, oral tradition, the emperor could not accomplish very much. Still, they believed—as do Jewish mystics today—that once you write the sacred Hebrew on the parchment the words take on a life of their own. Therefore, what could be done?

The scholars decided on this ingenious solution: every time that a name of God appeared in the Hebrew Bible, they would write it in gold ink. The emperor would regard this as an "enriched" version of their Bible—with all the fancy gold lettering. But, for the scholars, such a Bible would be spiritually voided and no longer powerful, for it had already violated the fundamental teaching that every letter must conform to Moses' version, in which all the letters were written in black ink.

This Greek translation of the Hebrew Bible has come to be known as the Septuagint. It became the basis for the way the world came to know the Bible, because all subsequent translations were made from it. Even the English translations that exist today are derived from the Septuagint, not from the Hebrew. In other words, all the translations of the Bible are several steps removed from the Hebrew—and to Kabbalists, as we shall see, this makes for some fundamental distortions and misinterpretations of God's revelation to Moses.

I can recommend a new translation of the Bible into English from the original Hebrew. It is called *The Living Torah* and was done by Rabbi Aryeh Kaplan, my own Kabbalistic teacher. It is as authentic a translation as you can find, and a very scholarly one. In addition to the translation, it has many maps, illustrations, and commentary.

It should also be emphasized that in the Hebrew Bible there are two sections that are very specific to the Kabbalah. For centuries they have been regarded as containing the Kabbalistic code in considerable detail. They concern the deepest mysteries of the universe. These two sections are the first chapter of Genesis and the first chapter of Ezekiel.

When you first turn to the Book of Ezekiel and examine the first chapter, the material appears very strange and nonsensical. Yet, this very strangeness—this "other-worldly" quality—is viewed as one of the holiest windows available to gaze into the transcendent world.

Of the Hebrew prophets, it is Ezekiel who most clearly describes the nature of the prophetic experience. He was one of the last prophets and he knew that much of what had been taught by word of mouth up to his day would cease to be transmitted. Therefore he wrote down in very precise terms what Kabbalists would regard as the full state of prophecy, though to outsiders it would seem quite bizarre.

In fact, Erich Van Däniken's book entitled *The Chariot of the Gods* (New York: Bantam, 1972) is based on Ezekiel's same vision. The author examines Ezekiel's account and concludes that it describes an encounter with—in current terminology—a UFO or spaceship. This is an interesting book, but the Kabbalistic interpretation has nothing to do with this modern effort to understand Ezekiel's powerful vision.

CHAPTER TWO

The Mystical Bible

Before examining the esoteric meaning of such key biblical sections as the Book of Ezekiel and Genesis 1, it is absolutely crucial to begin with the Kabbalistic premise that the Bible is of divine origin. Jewish mystics have for millennia taught that its every word and indeed its every letter is divine. Throughout the history of Judaism, the sages have emphasized that the words of the Bible are literally what God communicated to Moses at Mount Sinai. To this day, Orthodox Jews believe this principle without qualification; it is central to the esoteric path, too.

From this spiritual axiom, several principles immediately follow. First, every word of the Bible becomes very, very important. Moreover, each letter in every word becomes crucial; therefore, each word and letter imparts special significance. Second, there can be no real contradictions or mistakes in the Bible. Certainly, if the Bible is literally a communication from God, there can be no such errors. If passages or even phrases seem to be contradictory, Kabbalists insist that these can be reconciled with sufficient understanding of the text.

Third, the Bible is of eternal value to humanity. Flowing from the limitlessness of the Holy One, no aspect of the Bible can possibly become outdated or obsolete. Kabbalists deny the modern contention that the Bible merely reflects the particular worldview of one culture at one period in human history.

They emphatically reject the historical interpretation of the Bible, in which its message can be reduced to a particular epoch and culture.

Fourth, the Bible must be understood on many different levels simultaneously. Certainly one level can be taught as simple stories to children. But many other levels exist at the same time. Jewish mystics have long regarded the Bible as manifesting four different yet simultaneous levels of meaning. These are the plain meaning, the symbolic meaning, the allegorical meaning, and the esoteric meaning. For example, the Bible's opening phrase, "In the beginning", must be understood on each of these four levels to fully comprehend its divine message. Interestingly, some Kabbalists have said that only through understanding the deepest, esoteric strata of the Bible can we come to an accurate understanding of even its plain level—that we must "work backwards", in a sense, in biblical interpretation.

Fifth, the information conveyed by the Bible contains all potential knowledge in the universe. That is, within the narratives of the Bible are actually deeply hidden commentaries on the most recondite aspect of human existence and the cosmos. The Bible is seen to be a kind of "owner's manual" to the universe, with much specific instruction for personal development and growth.

How can this be? How can one work incorporate so much knowledge? An excellent model for helping us to see this is offered by modern genetics. Within each living cell is a nucleus and within the nucleus lies the genetic code for a particular organism. If we really understood the genetic code of the human species, we could reconstruct an entire person by utilizing the information in any one of his or her bodily cells.

Thus, in a very tiny space—the space occupied by a chromosome—an incredible amount of genetic information is stored. In theory, that microscopic space holds sufficient information for a whole creature to be created. Indeed, science today has already created or cloned very simple life forms. From this perspective, it is not so impossible for a single text—the Bible—to contain embedded within it vast information about the universe. And this notion brings us back to the

concept that the Bible is actually a God-given "owner's manual" to the cosmos.
Another point to bear in mind is that the original Hebrew Bible contains no chapter demarcations. To this day, it is just one long, continuous narrative. What happened historically is that when the Hebrew Bible was translated into Greek, non-Jewish scholars subdivided it into chapters to make more sense out of it. They sought to restructure the Hebrew Bible to make its form more consistent with other literary works of the time. These chapter subdivisions are therefore somewhat arbitrary. Certainly the Greek philosophers organized the material differently than did the Hebrew sages. The modern English translation of the Bible, of course, is based on the Greek, not on the Hebrew. For this reason, when we read the English Bible we inevitably come to a different reading than that intended by the Hebrew sages. When we later turn to Chapter One of Genesis, for example, we must realize that the original Hebrew ends this section at a different place than does the English version. To a Kabbalist, such seemingly minor deviations from the text become very significant.

SCIENCE AND THE KABBALAH

Before turning to some specific narratives in the Bible, it may first be helpful to examine from a Kabbalistic perspective the thorny issue of scientific versus religious truth. Certainly science and religion have been the two basic human forces that have changed the world. What is science? Science is really the use of the human intellect to obtain truth. This process has brought us many advantages throughout history. And what is religion as represented in Judaism by the Bible? Religion is the use of human spirituality to bring us closer to God.

Both science and religion ultimately derive from the Source of all. Therefore, science, the path of intellect, can bring us closer to God. In fact, the paths of science and religion are complementary; both are necessary for our complete development on the planet. The notion that the intellect must be combined with the spirit has long been fundamental to Judaism. From this perspective, its sages have long taught that there is only one ultimate truth and that there can be no contradiction between the Bible and science. If a conflict seems to exist, then the problem is seen to lie with current scientific knowledge, not with the Bible's account. Of course, people may also misunderstand what they read in the Bible. But with access to the secret, oral tradition of Judaism, the apparent contradictions or inconsistencies in the written Bible disappear.

Second, Judaism has emphasized that the realm of the physical world is very important. Even its most ardent mystics have taught that the only way we can draw closer to God is through the physical world; unlike some other spiritual teachers they have never sought to deny or denigrate the corporeal aspects of human life. Rather, they have always emphasized that we need a balance between the spiritual and the physical for harmonious life; or, in larger terms, that we need a balance between religion and science for a harmonious social order.

To be so entrenched in the Bible that we latch onto it in the most superficial manner is analogous to being without roots in the physical world. Yet to live in a world dominated by science without a concomitant spiritual sensitivity is analogous to a body without a soul. Today science dominates our lives to a tremendous extent; its worldview permeates our civilization. Consequently, when we examine the Bible and see statements that seem unscientific, our impulse is to reject the whole Bible as unsophisticated and outmoded. Kabbalists, though, say there is only one ultimate truth and that science and religion cannot possibly contradict one another.

For many of us, the Bible's seemingly outdated declaration that the universe was created in six days and that then God "rested" is a primary obstacle for believing the text literally. But Kabbalists teach that there can ultimately be no contradiction between modern subjects like astronomy or cosmology and the Bible. They insist that any apparent contradiction represents our own inability to penetrate the esoteric meaning of the sacred text. Therefore, there must be some way to understand the apparently outdated conceptions found in the Bible's account of Creation.

THE AGE OF THE UNIVERSE: THE SECRET TEACHING

How can we reconcile Genesis 1 with modern biological and cosmological evidence? Kabbalists believe that such a resolution has long existed, indeed since the very inception of the Bible. It was part of the hidden aspect of the Jewish oral tradition and it remained oral for millennia. However, approximately seven hundred years ago the Kabbalist Rabbi Isaac of Acco wrote down this ancient teaching. He disseminated such information precisely because modern science had begun to exist and he wished to create a harmony between these two paths of knowledge.

Rabbi Isaac of Acco was a genius. He knew the entire Bible by heart. He wrote a book called *The Treasury of Life*, a very secret manuscript. For many centuries it was studied only in manuscript form by select individuals drawn to Kabbalistic study. To this day it has never been published. In 1917 this manuscript was in Russia when the Bolsheviks seized power. The manuscript was stored in the rare manuscript section of the Lenin state Library. The curators knew that this was a very old manuscript but, because it had no title page, it was catalogued simply as a "six-hundred-year-old manuscript of unknown origin".

Kabbalists eventually began to search for the manuscript because they knew it had last been studied in Russia. Some time in the 1960s they located Rabbi Isaac's mystical treatise and sought to remove it from Russia—or at least examine it to determine its authenticity. However, Russian officials refused to let anyone even look at it. Finally one Kabbalist had a clever idea: he approached a publisher and told him that he needed this specific manuscript in researching his new book. The publisher agreed to contact the relevant Russian officials and eventually a copy of this mystical text was indeed sent—at considerable financial cost to the publisher and scholar. These are the events by which we now have access to Rabbi Isaac's centuries-old teaching concerning Genesis 1 and the age of the universe.

Rabbi Isaac's explanation is not difficult to grasp, but we must grasp it in a step-by-step process. He attributed this teaching ultimately to Moses himself at Mount Sinai. The key is the 90th Psalm, written by Moses. Indeed, Kabbalists regard Moses' 90th through 100th Psalms as comprising the hidden doorway to prophecy. The 90th Psalm says quite explicitly that a "God-day" corresponds to one thousand "man-years". Verse 4 declares, "For a thousand years in thy sight are but as yesterday..." This gives us one obvious clue. And there are several other major clues by which Jewish mystics arrive at their startling conclusion about the age of the universe. Let us examine these.

Genesis relates that the creation cycle consisted of seven days. In Judaism, the seven-year cycle is important. Every seventh year is a sabbatical year and historically that commandment had great significance. For example, the land had to stay fallow: it could not be farmed; no crops could be grown in the seventh years.

In Judaism, also, every seven-times-seven years, or forty-nine years, also represents something very significant: the jubilee year. Many laws exist concerning Jewish conduct during the jubilee year, such as pertaining to business and social relations. It is seen as the end of a specific sequence or cycle of events.

Kabbalists teach that there were also seven cycles of creation. Each cycle of creation is seen to have lasted seven thousand years—"man-years", that is. We are now living in the seventh cycle. Later in this book, when we examine teachings about the Messianic Age, this notion becomes quite important. But for now, let us mention the Kabbalistic belief that six cycles had already been completed before this current, seventh cycle. That is, all the events associated with Adam are seen to have occurred in the present cycle. And, only in the present cycle are "man-years" counted; before this cycle, the years are seen to refer to "God-years" only.

Since six cycles had been completed—each comprising seven thousand years—that corresponds to forty-two thousand "man-years". We have already related how the 90th Psalm explains that one "man-year" equals one "God-day". Therefore, one "God-year" equals 365,150 "man-years". So, if there were forty-two thousand "God-years" prior to Adam (six cycles of six thousand years each), that indicates the figure of

15,340,500,000 years. Remember, over seven hundred years ago Rabbi Isaac thus wrote that the universe is over fifteen billion years old. Because we are living in the seventh cycle, the Hebrew calendar simply records the number of years since Adam —or 5,746 years. But the total age of the universe, in Kabbalistic terms, is fifteen billion plus years, plus the 5,746 of our own cycle.

Ironically, Jewish mystics did not seek to publicly disseminate such information in the past because it would certainly have contradicted the state of scientific knowledge as it then existed. But such information today is remarkably consistent with current cosmological knowledge. By examining the speed by which astronomical bodies in the universe are hurtling apart from one another, scientists have been able to approximate the number of years that date from the original "Big Bang" when everything was created out of an infinitesimally small point.

This little exercise is simply one way to dramatize the notion that there can be no ultimate contradiction between science and religion as represented by the Bible in Judaism. Both arrive at the same truth through different means. The fact that a Kabbalistic manuscript written more than seven hundred years ago calculated the age of the universe as approximately fifteen billion years bears powerful witness to this principle.

It is striking to note too that this Kabbalistic teaching comments on some of the specific changes within the evolutionary process—changes that took place before the last shift or mutation—involving other forms of life on the planet. That is, Jewish mystics have for millennia insisted that God created many worlds besides this one, and that this heavenly process occurred one thousand times. This notion is quite intriguing, that an evolutionary process happened and then abruptly shifted or "mutated" one thousand different times.

Thus, when the Kabbalah states the universe is fifteen billion years old, and that one thousand evolutionary "shifts" occurred, it is clearly intimating that a change occurred once every fifteen million years. We are also told that the last of such changes occurred with the advent of Adam—5,746 years ago, according to the Jewish calendar. We can therefore conclude that the last evolutionary shift or mutation happened fifteen million years before Adam, or fifteen million plus 5,746 years in the past.

In that distant era, primordial man arose. The evolutionary shift may have involved a variety of aspects, but the crucial point, the Kabbalah teaches, is that before then only a kind of prehuman creature existed. This notion does not necessarily indicate that Darwin's account of evolution is the most accurate; there are many challenges to it within the field of biology today. However, this concept certainly suggests a Kabbalistic belief in some sort of evolutionary process at work in our planet's history.

Why has such fascinating and potentially explosive information not become better known to people today? Perhaps one reason is that those who have access to Jewish mystical wisdom are not eager for publicity; they have been content to study quietly and to know their material in a personally uplifting way. Not everyone nowadays is hungry for media prominence. Another reason is that not all people today would even accept this interpretation of the Bible, since it derives strongly from the Jewish Oral Tradition. Certainly Christian fundamentalists deny the legitimacy of this Tradition, for clearly the Kabbalah offers a very different perspective on the Bible—and on material we may have thought we knew well for years.

THE PURPOSE OF GENESIS 1

To really understand anything significant about the opening chapter of the Bible it is first necessary to ask: what is its purpose? What is the divine intent behind this perplexing material? Clearly the purpose is not scientific. It may resemble scientific discourse for some people, but it is not really scientific discourse. At the same time, this narrative is certainly not historically oriented. If we were to record the early history of the planet, we surely could write a better account. Nor can we attribute the content of Genesis 1 to an intention of presenting a synopsis. If we accept the axiom that God wrote the Bible, and transmitted it to Moses at Mount Sinai, then we must acknowledge that the Holy One had no need to give only a summary.

Jewish mystics teach that the first chapter of Genesis is meant neither as a scientific nor as an historical account. This notion does not mean that Genesis contradicts science or history, but that its purpose is quite different from such modern fields of study. Kabbalists say that its purpose is to offer a spiritual statement; this view is consistent with their concept that the Bible is a spiritual handbook to enable us to become closer to God. By better comprehending this account of creation, they have long insisted, we learn how to draw nearer to God.

How does the story of creation relate to our present lives? This issue touches on a fundamental Kabbalistic premise: that creation is an ongoing process. Jewish mystics teach that creation did not merely happen some time in the distant past, but that it continues through every instant of the universe's existence. Unlike some religious traditions that regard creation as something that God did once and then withdrew from; Judaism has for millennia emphasized that the divine flow continues unending at every moment. If for one instant God were to withdraw the smallest aspect of His Being from our cosmos, everything would cease to exist. All would revert back to the undifferentiated and trans-infinite nature of the *Ain Sof.* Everything that exists does so because God originally created it and because God's creative flow continues to sustain that object.

This concept is a primary tenet of Jewish philosophy and is central to the Kabbalah. In the same way this esoteric system teaches that a bridge connects man and God, and continues to exist in the creative flow between them. The same creative force that was utilized in creating the universe is utilized in sustaining it at every instant. If we can attune ourselves to this creative force, we have a bridge—a pathway— between ourselves and God. Therefore, if we truly understand the divine flow described in Genesis, we possess knowledge to bring ourselves closer to the Holy One.

From this perspective, we can regard the entire narrative of Creation as a form of meditation. The Bible seeks to give us a spiritual message to draw nearer to God. This message relates to our learning to connect to these forces of creation. Thus, we can see the whole seven-day episode recounted in Genesis as constituting a very specific prescription for meditation; this is in part how Kabbalists have traditionally used this material. Bear in mind, though, that such an approach does not negate the other ways to approach the Bible. A fundamental Kabbalistic premise is that every line and indeed every word of the Bible can be understood simultaneously on many levels of meaning.

CAN THE HEBREW BIBLE BE TRANSLATED

Before turning to specific passages of the Bible and their mystical interpretation, it is important to bear in mind several points concerning the issue of translation. First, it is virtually a truism to say that whenever we translate from one language to another—no matter how excellent the effort—something becomes lost. The poetry and the nuance often fall away. This observation holds true even for translation from earlier English into modern English, such as in reading Shakespeare's work. In translating Hebrew into English, therefore, much of the subtlety and nuance become lost.

However, for Jewish mystics, the problem runs far deeper. For millennia, they have taught that every letter's shape, sound, and numerical value contain esoteric information that completely transcends the specific, contextual meaning of the word. There is really no way at all to translate these three factors into any other language, English or otherwise. Even the most literal translation of the Hebrew word into English inevitably loses these three other characteristics which convey the more hidden information in coded form.

This issue is precisely why the Bible's mystical significance is very difficult to apprehend without a thorough knowledge of Hebrew. To practice Kabbalistic spiritual exercises is not such a difficult matter; Hebrew is not essential for all of these. But to really understand the metaphysical basis for the Kabbalah without being able to read the Hebrew Bible—that is a very different matter.

THE BOOK OF EZEKIEL

Let us now examine the first chapter of the Book of Ezekiel. It is important to know that historically Kabbalists have regarded this section of the Bible, together with the first chapter of Genesis, as providing the keys to human existence and our relation to the universe. Traditionally, this aspect of Jewish mysticism has been known as *Ma'aseh Merkabah* ("The Act of the Divine Chariot").

The first significant line to comprehend in the Book of Ezekiel is Chapter 1:28, actually the last line of the first chapter. Ezekiel relates, "I fell upon my face, and I heard the voice of one speaking." This line reveals the whole purpose of what Ezekiel has just recounted—that he has undergone the prophetic experience. He has been through a detailed process that leads to the experience mentioned in the last line of the chapter: "And I heard the voice of one speaking." In other words, the many details that Ezekiel sets forth in Chapter 1, strange and enigmatic as they seem, are the specific steps necessary to achieve prophetic consciousness.

The actual text of Ezekiel 1 reads as follows:

IN THE THIRTIETH YEAR, IN THE fourth month, on the fifth day of the month, as I was among the exiles by the river Chebar, the heavens were opened, and I saw visions of God. 2On the fifth day of the month (it was the fifth year of the exile of King Jehoi'achin), 3the word of the LORD came to Ezekiel the priest, the son of Buzi, in the land of the Chalde'ans by the river Chebar; and the hand of the LORD was upon him there.

4 As I looked, behold, a stormy wind came out of the north, and a great cloud, with brightness round about it, and fire flashing forth continually, and in the midst of the fire, as it were gleaming bronze. 5And from the midst of it came the likeness of four living creatures. And this was their appearance: they had the form of men, 6but each had four faces, and each of them had four wings. 7Their legs were straight, and the soles of their feet were like the sole of a calf's foot; and they sparkled like burnished bronze. 8Under their wings on their four sides they had human hands. And the four had their faces and their wings thus: 9 their wings touched one another; they went every one straight forward, without turning as they went. 10As for the likeness of their

faces, each had the face of a man in front; the four had the
face of a lion on the right side, the four had the face of an
ox on the left side, and the four had the face of an eagle at
the back. [11]Such were their faces. And their wings were
spread out above; each creature had two wings, each of which
touched the wing of another, while two covered their bodies.
[12]And each went straight forward; wherever the spirit
would go, they went, without turning as they went. [13]In the
midst of the living creatures there was something that
looked like burning coals of fire, like torches moving to and
fro among the living creatures; and the fire was bright and
out of the fire went forth lightning. [14]And the living creatures darted to and fro, like a flash of lightning.

15   Now as I looked at the living creatures, I saw a
wheel upon the earth beside the living creatures, one for
each of the four of them. [16]As for the appearance of the
wheels and their construction: their appearance was like the
gleaming of a chrysolite; and the four had the same likeness, their construction being as it were a wheel within a
wheel. [17]When they went, they went in any of their four
directions without turning as they went. [18]The four wheels
had rims and they had spokes; and their rims were full of eyes
round about. [19]And when the living creatures went, the
wheels went beside them; and when the living creatures rose
from the earth, the wheels rose. [20]Wherever the spirit would
go, they went, and the wheels rose along with them; for the
spirit of the living creatures was in the wheels. [21]When
those went, these went; and when those stood, these stood;
and when those rose from the earth, the wheels rose along
with them; for the spirit of the living creatures was in the
wheels.

22   Over the heads of the living creatures there was the
likeness of a firmament, shining like crystal, spread out
above their heads. [23]And under the firmament their wings
were stretched out straight, one toward another; and each
creature had two wings covering its body. [24]And when they
went, I heard the sound of their wings like the sound of many
waters, like the thunder of the Almighty, a sound of tumult
like the sound of a host; when they stood still, they let down
their wings. [25]And there came a voice from above the firmament over their heads; when they stood still, they let down
their wings.

26   And above the firmament over their heads there
was the likeness of a throne, in appearance like sapphire; and
seated above the likeness of a throne was a likeness as it were
of a human form. [27]And upward from what had the appearance of his loins I saw as it were gleaming bronze, like the
appearance of fire enclosed round about; and downward from

what had the appearance of his loins I saw as it were the appearance of fire, and there was brightness round about him.
[28]Like the appearance of the bow that is in the cloud on the day of rain, so was the appearance of the brightness round about.
Such was the appearance of the likeness of the glory of the LORD. And when I saw it, I fell upon my face, and I heard the voice of one speaking.(Oxford Annotated Bible, 1962.)

It is quite likely that if this narrative were not contained in the Bible, the most sacred text for the West, we would pay very little attention to it. Yet, some of the wisest thinkers in Judaism have for millennia regarded this account as containing the secrets of the universe. They have insisted though that we must be able to penetrate behind the surface meaning of the words, for even an accurate knowledge of Hebrew will otherwise be of little help to us.

Jewish mystics have offered several intriguing concepts concerning this mysterious section of the Bible. First, they have related that chapter one of the Book of Ezekiel describes the specific methodology for the achievement of prophecy. How is it then that this description is not offered anywhere else in the Bible? Why was Ezekiel the only prophet to reveal such information? Several reasons have been handed down through the centuries.

To begin with, Kabbalists explain that Ezekiel was a rather unsophisticated mystic. He recounted his experience in such detail because, in a way, he was so overwhelmed by its newness and power. Think of a rural man today who had never left his remote village in Africa or Asia—and who is suddenly transported to New York City's Grand Central Station with its hundreds of passenger lines. In describing his train journey in a letter, the villager might well begin by relating, "I came to a huge station filled with many bright lights that flashed throughout the building. Some lights flashed with red color, others with green or yellow. The vehicles moved incredibly swiftly as their doors shut tightly. The men and women inside sat or moved slowly from side to side. . ." The whole first section of the villager's letter concerning his train ride might recount his impressions of Grand Central Station.

By this analogy, we arrive at one explanation that is traditional among Kabbalists concerning Ezekiel's account. They have long contended that his prophetic experience was precisely the same as that of all the other prophets; there was nothing unique about it. The Talmud—certainly a nonmystical work—explicitly comments that Ezekiel experienced what all prophets did before the onset of their specific revelations from God. That is why the sages viewed Ezekiel as rather unsophisticated; unlike the other prophets, he felt the need to record the nature of the preparatory aspects of prophetic consciousness. This is one explanation traditionally offered; it is not universally accepted in Judaism, though.

A second explanation concerning the content of the Book of Ezekiel's first chapter is that Ezekiel was thereby seeking Jewish acceptance of his prophecy. Remember, he was in Babylon, not in the Land of Israel, when he experienced this vision. His people had been exiled from the Land of Israel, primarily to Babylon. Ezekiel was in a foreign country, and it was rare for divine revelations to come to Jews in such places. Therefore, one interpretation that Kabbalists have long advanced is that he was trying to substantiate the authenticity of his prophecy. One way for him to accomplish this task was to insert it in the first chapter, because all those who knew from the Oral Tradition the nature of prophecy would immediately recognize that Ezekiel had indeed attained the prophetic state.

One might ask: were not others in Ezekiel's vicinity when he underwent his vision? If so, could not they confirm what he witnessed? Kabbalists teach that such experiences manifest themselves on other levels of human consciousness; if other people were in Ezekiel's immediate vicinity, they would have seen nothing. In fact, the Book of Daniel provides a very clear description of Daniel's vision and specifically indicates that those physically near him saw nothing at all out of the ordinary.

There is yet a third, quite reasonable explanation on this issue. Some Jewish mystics point to the oral teaching that there would be a period of one thousand years—from the moment of Moses' vision of the burning bush onward—when divine prophecy would be available to humanity. Ezekiel was one of the last prophets. He knew that this mystical epoch was about to end and that some of the Oral Tradition might become lost. Therefore, to preserve some of this esoteric wisdom for the coming age of spiritual darkness, he wrote down this knowledge. For he knew that the subsequent age would last thousands of years without the benefit of divine communication. Not wishing to make readily accessible potentially dangerous information, though, Ezekiel wrote it in code. In those last days of prophecy, there were three prophets who were alive and, as mentioned earlier, they all died within one month of one another. Thus the era of divine prophecy ended. By Jewish calendar reckoning, this period corresponded to the years 2448 to 3448.

Why did Ezekiel seek to keep such information restricted? We have already seen the analogy of the esoteric wisdom to sticks of dynamite. Dynamite can be very constructive; it can help build roads and bridges. But we would not give sticks of dynamite to kindergarten children, however great their eagerness to build roads and bridges. This material was quite explosive, and Ezekiel perceived the need to protect it from those who might misuse it on purpose or out of ignorance. Interestingly, the Book of Ezekiel is not the only section of the Bible where prophetic techniques are described in code. Tradition has it that when Moses ascended Mount Sinai to convene with the Holy One, he passed through ten spiritual realms. At each level, he offered a psalm and these ten psalms—the 90th through 99th—have been seen to recount in code the steps to achieve prophetic consciousness.

CHAPTER THREE

In the Beginning

AIN SOF: THE NATURE OF GOD

It is crucial to know that Kabbalists have a very special word for "God". The time-honored Hebrew term is known as *Ain Sof*. Literally, that means "without end" or "eternal". This is the name that Jewish mystics employ in thinking about God. The concept of the *Ain Sof* is very important in the Kabbalah; one reason is that the Bible contains different names of God and that each Name is understood very specifically.

What is *Ain Sof*? To begin with, it is important to be aware that the term *Ain Sof* does not even appear in the Bible. Other divine Names are mentioned—such as *Elokim*—but not *Ain Sof*. To Kabbalists, this indicates that the actual Name of God appears nowhere in the Bible; the other Names are not references to God. In English translations of the Bible, the word "God" is used over and over; but in the Hebrew version, different words are used in different places in the Bible—never *Ain Sof*.

Jewish mystics regard *Ain Sof* as something utterly beyond human comprehension. That has to be the starting point for all Kabbalistic thinking about God—that *Ain Sof* is completely transcendent of human language. There is literally nothing we can meaningfully say about *Ain Sof*. One cannot start a sentence with the word "God" and complete it with anything meaningful. For example, we cannot meaningfully say, "God is good," because God totally transcends our limited concepts of good and evil. God is without limits. The moment we declare, "God is . . ." the sentence loses its meaning, because God is without limits.

The vivid Kabbalistic analogy for this notion is the image of a fist holding a thought: just as it is impossible for a fist to hold a thought, the human mind cannot hold the concept of God. Why is it that a fist cannot hold a thought? The reason, of course, has nothing to do with how strong the fist is. We can go to a health club and build up our muscles, but no matter how strong we make the fist, it will never hold a thought. This is because a fist exists on one level or plane of reality, and a thought exists on a totally different plane. They are both real enough; a thought is real and a fist is real. But they exist in two different realms and there is no way that we can reach in with the fist to the world of thought and grab anything. In a like manner, it is simply impossible for the human mind to grasp the concept of God or *Ain Sof*.

This conclusion now leads us to an interesting issue: is God spiritual? Clearly, if we asked whether God is physical, the answer would be negative. But is God spiritual? Kabbalists say no, God is as different from the spiritual as God is from the physical. The same distance that separates God from the physical must separate God from the spiritual. Kabbalists definitely emphasize that many other planes exist besides ours and that many spiritual beings inhabit such realms. But this fact has nothing to do with the concept of *Ain Sof* and our inherent inability to comprehend it.

This compelling notion can best be understood by way of analogy, and several analogies are available to us. For example, think of the sun. On a bright day, it is literally impossible for us to look directly at the sun without an intervening shield like sunglasses. The human eye cannot gaze at that type of brightness. Furthermore, there is a certain distance that we must keep from the sun. If a human started to approach it, he could get only within a certain number of million miles before physically evaporating. Yet the same sun is just one medium-sized star among billions of stars that science has identified. If the power and magnitude of a medium-sized star is so great, then star is so great, then clearly, the power of *Ain Sof* is so incomprehensibly immense that a vast, vast distance must by necessity separate it from each of us. To retain our separate identities, we must exist at a certain great distance from *Ain Sof* or we must employ a shield like sunglasses. Another analogy relates to the electricity that we use in our homes. The electricity may be produced at a power plant that produces some half a million volts of charge. The wires running from the plant carry this half a million charge of volts. Such a charge cannot possibly be brought into a line to a house because it would burn the house down. To make usable the volts produced by the power plant, it is necessary to have a series of step-down points. In this way, the large energy is distributed from a central area and reduced to fifty thousand volts; from there, in turn, it is further reduced to smaller and smaller units. Finally the unit is small enough so that a wire can run into a house and be safely utilized. The basic notion is that the original energy source is simply too powerful for ordinary use and that it must be reduced gradually through a series of steps.

A third analogy about *Ain Sof* can be offered. Think of radioactive material, which cannot be directly handled. Some intervening system is necessary to handle it. By employing mechanical arms, we can make safe use of the material; to touch such a substance directly would be suicidal.

These analogies begin to help us to comprehend that the power of *Ain Sof* is not only beyond all human conception but also beyond our capacity to withstand. A system comprising a step-down arrangement between *Ain Sof* and the human individual must exist between our separate identities. With such a step-down system, communication between *Ain Sof* and human individuals can take place. This form of communication would be indirect, of course, since many step-down stations would be involved.

The Kabbalah teaches that precisely such a step-down system exists: that ten spheres of energy called *sefiroth* emanate from *Ain Sof* down to our realm. According to Kabbalistic tradition, only seven *sefiroth* are accessible to humans; three are inaccessible. Above these higher three *sefiroth* are a number of steps leading to *Ain Sof.*

It is not hard to imagine how historically people have come to regard the *sefiroth* as akin to gods. In one section of the Bible we are told that men and women began to call upon the names of God to achieve certain ends. These people understood quite well the relationship between the *sefiroth* and power, because the ten forces they comprise create and sustain everything in the universe. Certainly it is easy to see how individuals might start to treat a *sefirah* as a god—to deify, worship, and pay homage to it. Perhaps this outlook underlay the early notion that a multiplicity of gods ruled the cosmos.

Several examples can be offered to illustrate this aspect of esoteric Jewish thought. For instance, God instructs the Jewish people not to make idols. However, the Holy One also tells them to build two idols—in the form of cherubs—in the holiest place within their entire religious focus: the sacred ark containing the Ten Commandments. Kabbalists explain this seeming contradiction by pointing to God's statement, "I will speak to you from between these cherubs." In other words, the cherubs were foci for the transmission of prophecy.

The Kabbalistic principle, then, is that idols can really be effective, but they must not be worshipped as independent deities. If idols were not effective, there would have been no need for God to prohibit their worship. People in those days were not so ignorant as we often think; in some ways, they had greater spiritual awareness than we do in our highly materialist and technological age.

The ancients hardly believed that they could take a block of stone, carve something onto it, and thereby create a god. The Egyptian civilization was able to accomplish many astounding feats, some of which we cannot even duplicate today. It is incomprehensible that these same people could believe that their blocks of stone were really God. Yet this notion is what modern educators promulgate: that the ancient Egyptians built the pyramids, practiced sophisticated embalming and the like, and simultaneously believed that these stones were God. This popular, modern view is completely wrong.

The ancient statues were essentially devices for focusing human awareness during meditation. They were designed to bring people to altered states of consciousness in various ways. Many means exist to reach this goal today, such as crystal balls and Tarot cards; many techniques exist by which one can attain a certain level of awareness. The ancients practiced a very sophisticated system—resembling a "science" in our own terminology—in their use of statues to elevate human consciousness. This system was very advanced, and it worked.

The Jewish mystical tradition has for millennia prohibited such paths precisely because they are effective. Kabbalists have never denied that such methods work; however, they have banned their use as intrinsic violations of the Jewish approach to the Divine. That is why the utilization of statues as intermediaries is prohibited.

The Biblical account of the Golden Calf is an illustration of the Jewish attitude toward idols. Initially, the entire narrative seems quite bizarre. After several hundred years of enslavement, the Jewish people were liberated from their bondage in the most miraculous manner. Indeed, the Bible asserts that this liberation was the greatest manifestation of God's power on earth that had ever taken place or will ever take place. These Jews witnessed the liberation themselves; it was not something they read about. They experienced the parting of the sea; they experienced one miracle after another. They were given perceptions of the Holy One. Following this whole series of events, Moses announced to them that he was going up Mount Sinai to receive the final messages from God, and that then he would return to them.

Moses ascended Mount Sinai, announcing he would return in forty days. The Oral Tradition then relates that a controversy arose among the people as to whether he had been gone forty or forty-one days. Believing that forty-one days had elapsed—one day beyond the appointed time—the people thereupon formed a Golden Calf. The Bible recounts that they took their gold, fashioned the Calf, and began to pray to it.

If we had witnessed such miracles just a short while before, would we make a Golden Calf because of one day's difference? Kabbalists insist that we must view this account in another context to understand what was really occurring then. Their notion is quite antithetical to the modern interpretation that the Jewish people—out of frustration and superstition—felt impelled to worship an idol. Rather, Kabbalists suggest that the Jewish people were quite spiritually advanced at that time; they knew a great deal about spiritual powers and how to achieve heightened inner states. By forming the Golden Calf, they were not attempting to reject God but to reach Him through another path, that practiced by the Egyptians.

From this perspective, the Jewish people in the desert knew very well how to create devices for focusing consciousness during meditation. To use a modern analogy, one can think of such devices as radio receivers: if various wires are connected in certain ways, suddenly one begins to hear voices emanating from a little box. Similarly, the Jewish people knew how to build spiritual "receivers" to tune in to the transcendent world. By making the Golden Calf, they were building a very powerful "receiver", through which to reach God.

The heavenly prohibition was not that such a method would lead them to the wrong place spiritually; it was that such methods would cause them to face certain consequences. The paths were not by their nature sacrilegious or evil; but God had commanded them not to take those paths, such as that of the Egyptians. The Kabbalah teaches that the Egyptian culture was steeped in such techniques; Moses himself knew them intimately, for he had been raised as a prince in the Pharoah's palace.

The sacrilege of the Jewish people, then, was in choosing the Egyptian means over that which God had given to them. Such conduct constituted a direct violation of God's commandment. The Jewish people were not seeking to defy the Holy One by forming the Golden Calf, but they had definitely disregarded the commandment. Indeed, a certain segment of the Jewish population warned the majority against trying to reach God in this way.

The Bible makes clear that such idol worship represented the human effort to come closer to God. Through the Prophet Haggai, God says that all idol worship everywhere—whether Jewish or non-Jewish—is an attempt to reach him. The issue is that certain paths are prohibited.

Why did God ban certain paths? The Kabbalah teaches that human logic cannot comprehend such matters. The Jewish mystics declare that in certain instances, such as this one, the meta-logic of *Ain Sof* is involved, and that we are simply unable to make sense of the reasons. Can one try to reason with a two-year-old who is dashing onto a highway to retrieve his ball? Not there, at that moment: one must simply prohibit such behavior. We are seen to be like the two-year-old in this situation and therefore elaborate explanations are not offered to us.

A whole system of communication was established between *Ain Sof* and man. This communication system can be understood in at least two different ways. The first involves the multiple worlds or universes. There are at least five universes; many Kabbalistic sources mention four, but there is a fifth which is far less discussed. There are five universes that intervene between *Ain Sof* and this world, this planet, and this galaxy as we understand these.

Each of these universes is a step-down station for the power of *Ain Sof* until finally it flows into our universe. In this way, we can use this unimaginable force so that it will not destroy us. As we look at each of the five universes in turn, bear in mind that the basic function of each is to provide some type of step-down system. Therefore, the fact that Genesis 1 mentions light five times is hardly a coincidence. Each allusion to light relates to one of the five universes. Each one is really a meditative key to understanding that universe, too.

There is also a second way to view this divine communication system, one equally important. It is to adopt the perspective that there were certain basic forces employed in Creation. It is as if *Ain Sof* set up certain basic spiritual forces and these forces—through their own being and intelligence—proceeded to form the universe. Now, there were ten of these forces. Remember, the word *Ain Sof* never appears in the Bible. Rather, there are ten different Names of God and Kabbalistically each is representative of one of these ten basic forces.

Each of these forces has its own characteristics; each is somewhat different from the others. Therefore, when a specific *Sefirah* is mentioned, it is because of its unique attributes. That specific Name of God is mentioned because of a particular manifestation of the Divine occurring at that moment.

THE TREE OF LIFE

A central symbol of the Kabbalah is the Tree of Life. If you look at the diagram on page 179, you can see ten circles. They can be lined up in different ways. The entire concept of the Tree of Life depends on an understanding of the ten *Sefiroth*.

The first principle to know is that each *Sefirah* is a basic force, a particular manifestation of the deity. This notion immediately addresses an old criticism of the Bible which questions all the descriptions of God becoming angry with the Jews, His threats of vengeance, His causing of many terrible events and disasters. The God of the Bible seems to be a very vengeful, angry God, and not a God of love. But what are we really talking about?

Kabbalists insist that we are not talking about *Ain Sof*, because *Ain Sof* is mentioned nowhere in the Bible. Rather, we are talking about some of the forces. It is clear that this may be so, because the notion that God gets angry is ludicrous when you think about it. Think of the scenario if God gets angry. It means that if I do something "bad", then God gets angry at me. If this is true, then I possess tremendous power; I am virtually in control of God. I can make Him happy and I can make Him angry, and I can make Him sad. I can make His day and I can break His day.

Obviously, that kind of God is not a very powerful God if He is so dependent on what I do for His emotional response. When we really think of the implications of this popular portrayal of God, it is ludicrous. An all-powerful, all-knowing deity cannot be so vulnerable and dependent on what I do. There are billions of people on our planet, each doing a variety of deeds. How could such a God possibly have a good day?

God would clearly be rather foolish to give that power to any one of us, let alone to all of us. To think of a God who becomes angry as a result of human behavior is really to misunderstand what God is all about. Now, the *Sefiroth* are not God. God designed them in such a way so that they can be understood by the human model. Or, to put matters in another way, human logic is based on these ten forces. Each of them contributes to the macrocosm of the universe; each contributes to the microcosm of the human mind. Thus we have the capability to comprehend these ten forces.

One way to view these forces is therefore to look at man: each of us is a reflection of the larger microcosm. Indeed, this Kabbalistic concept can be seen in the Biblical line in which man's creation is described. The text reads, "Let us make man in our image." This is a very strange line; who does "us" refer to? The line clearly says "our" image. Jewish mystics understand this passage to indicate that *Elokim*—one of the *Sefiroth* —is saying to the other *Sefiroth*, "Let us make man in our image." The purpose was to create man as a microcosm of the *Sefiroth* so that we would possess the ability to understand them.

Therefore, our emotional life—for example, our capacity to become angry—is a reflection of the *Sefiroth*. This does not imply that one *Sefirah* manifests only anger; the Kabbalah is much more complex than that. But certainly one component of one particular *Sefirah* is seen in human anger. Indeed, all of what we call the human emotions are aspects of the *Sefiroth*. Kabbalists suggest that the emotions are there because they exist in the *Sefiroth*. Our emotionality constitutes a reflection of the *Sefiroth*.

As a corollary to this principle, we can say that the *Sefiroth* respond in a way similar to that of human beings. Or, conversely, man responds in a way similar to that of the *Sefiroth*. The forces are such that they can respond in ways that would seem like anger or love. But despite their awesome power, the *Sefiroth* are not God—*Ain Sof*—and should never be confused with God.

GENESIS 1: AN OVERVIEW

Before we can understand anything about this first chapter of the Bible, we must ask: what is its purpose? Here, we are given a description of how the world supposedly began. But is this really the Bible's intent? Obviously we are not being presented with a scientific discourse on how the world began. This description may resemble the language of scientific discourse, but it hardly meets such criteria if this were the aim. At the same time, the first chapter of the Bible is not a very good historical or chronological narrative. What, then, is God's purpose in transmitting this material to us?

Jewish mystics have for many centuries agreed that Genesis 1 is intended neither as a scientific nor as an historical statement. By acknowledging this, however, they have nevertheless insisted that Genesis 1 cannot ultimately deny science or history. Rather, they have seen this enigmatic section of the Bible as representing a spiritual statement, whose purpose is to help bring us closer to God.

We must begin then to approach the material from this perspective: that the account of creation in some way can enable us to draw closer to the Holy One. But what relevance does the narrative of creation have for this effort? Even if we accept the Kabbalistic premise that God generated certain forces of creation for the cosmos to exist, how does that pertain to our personal lives? The answer lies in the fundamental Kabbalistic notion that creation is an ongoing process.

Jewish sages have long taught that creation was not an event that happened once in the unimaginable past and then ended. They have instead argued that the universe exists at this very moment—and at every moment—because the Holy One wills that celestial flow to continue. God's inconceivable energy creates the cosmos anew at every tiniest billionth-to-the-billionth of a second. If God for one instant withdrew His Being from our universe, everything—from the greatest galaxies to the smallest subatomic particles—would cease to exist. All would revert back to the *Ain Sof*.

From this compelling concept it follows that the creative flow described in Genesis 1 did not end in the distant past but continues at this moment. Kabbalists declare that the bridge between God and man still exists in the creative flow emanating from the *Ain Sof* at every instant. Therefore, by attuning ourselves to this heavenly flow, we can bring ourselves closer to God.

The forces that link us to God are the channels we must cross to reach Him. This is the basic concept to bear in mind. Thus, there is something in the narrative of the first seven days of creation that will explain the nature of these channels to be crossed. From this perspective, the entire account of creation is a meditative device; it provides a spiritual message for connecting to these forces. Indeed, Kabbalists indicate that we can link ourselves meditatively to these celestial forces; that each description in the text radiates a specific detail pertaining to meditation.

Nevertheless, to approach Genesis 1 as a meditative text does not negate its other levels of meaning. Kabbalists believe that there are many, many levels to the Bible and that all are valid and important to its complete comprehension as God's message for us.

MYSTERIES OF GENESIS 1

Let us explore now some of the specific content of the first chapter of Genesis, by taking an example from the account of the first day. What was created on the first day? Light was created. How many times is the word "light" mentioned concerning that first day? It is mentioned five times. And from this point onward, Kabbalists become very precise in understanding the text.

Remember, if God authored the Bible, then He hardly needed to be redundant. Why five times, then? What is the significance of five? Kabbalists always regard numbers as very important; some aspects of creation are mentioned three times, others ten times. Be aware, too, that although the English word "light" is used in the modern Bible, Jewish mystics do not think of this energy as akin to anything with which we are familiar in everyday life. For example, the Bible clearly states that the sun had not yet been formed.

Let us identify the various references to light in this section. These are:

1) "God said, 'There shall be light.' "
2) "Light came."*
3) "God saw the light."
4) "God divided light and darkness."
5) "God named the light."

This progression of events is quite intriguing. The first reference suggests that there was a moment in time when light did not yet exist. It was not even manifest in the divine realm. The second step recounts that light came; it became manifest. However, it could not be seen. This intimates that the light had no physical reality yet. It was a nonphysical process. This second point is implying, then, that existence may transcend our perceptual abilities. We can also interpret this reference to suggest that there can be a moment when a thought exists in the human mind before it is expressed outwardly in any way.

Step three relates that "God saw the light." That statement is a bit strange to ponder because we cannot see light. We can see things that light bounces off; we see with light, we see in light, but we do not see light itself. Another interesting aspect of this step is that the phrase "And God said" first appears in the text.

The fourth step recounts that "God divided the light from the darkness." But where has darkness been mentioned? Which comes first: light or darkness? This reference intimates that darkness already existed and therefore preceded the creation of light. For Kabbalists, this concept is very important; it touches on other issues like: what does darkness represent? Ignorance? Evil? Apparently darkness precedes light in the account of creation.

Also, the question immediately arises: to God, what is the distinction between darkness and light? Obviously, these are not physical references; the Bible is hardly suggesting that God cannot see in the dark. Jewish mystics insist that this entire account is designed to heighten human spirituality;

*In some translations this becomes:
1) "Let there be light."
2) "There was light."

therefore, we must consider what this reference is really teaching us. For instance, we know that "God saw that the light was good." Thus, the distinction between darkness and light is relevant to our own existence.

Be aware that Kabbalists say that darkness was not the only thing that was created before light. Heaven and earth were created first. There was heaven, then there was earth, and then the Bible alludes to darkness.

The fifth and last step narrates that God named the light. This statement tells us something regarding that famous question, "What's in a name?" This reference indicates that names are indeed quite important. God gives things names. Somehow, then, the last step in the process of creation is to name that which has been created. Kabbalists view this step as describing the significance of naming for our own involvement in creating things.

This step also suggests that we—in a universe filled with names—are at the bottom of this five-step process of creation. If we wish to come closer to God, then we must work our way up the five-step ladder to Him.

Kabbalists thus indicate that the main purpose of the account of Creation is to help us attune our mind to the forces of Creation. Why is this so important? Because, for the Kabbalists, Creation is an ongoing process; it is happening right now. They have long regarded these forces as the connecting link between the Creator and the created—plants, stones, animals, and human beings. Therefore, if we can properly align ourselves with the celestial forces, then we possess a link back to God. The entire narrative of Creation can be viewed in a meditative context. That is, it actually provides sophisticated instructions on how to meditate. The references to "light" in Genesis 1 can certainly be seen from this perspective.

Let us see what this really entails. Our first step is to name something. Helen Keller, for example, possessed much conceptual knowledge but did not begin to function normally until she could say "water"and name what her senses communicated. Once we can name something, we can truly focus on it; we have a point of meditation. And this act brings us to our second level: being able to "divide the light from the darkness".

This reference suggests that our second step is to separate or demarcate a thing from that which is different. The third level is where "God saw the light" or "saw that it was good". This is the level when meditatively we see the divine goodness.

The fourth level—counting upwards, of course, from our own—is the level where duality is transcended. This is the level before the light could be seen; there was not yet any differentiation between darkness and light. Jewish mysticism teaches that behind the duality of the universe is an eternal oneness. As a vivid example of this notion, think of a beautiful diamond and also a piece of excrement. Is there any difference between them? Superficially, there is tremendous difference; we all can see it plainly. But at the submolecular level of their atomic structures, there is virtually no distinction at all. Both are comprised of atoms and whirling electrons.

Even in physical reality, therefore, there is a level when these two substances are the same. But Kabbalists posit a much higher realm where the connectedness of everything exists. They suggest that the Biblical reference to this level can help bring us through meditation to this exalted state of awareness.

The fifth and highest level is that of God or the *Ain Sof.* Before there was light, there was God. When we ascend these earlier levels, we come to the level of God. However, Jewish mysticism never suggests that we can merge completely with God; we can come very close but some distance must remain. Certainly, this interesting notion partly distinguishes the Kabbalah from other spiritual traditions.

The Secret Code of the Hebrew Letters

On the same subject of light in Genesis 1, an important aspect of Kabbalistic teaching emerges. That is, every Hebrew letter is associated with a specific numerical value. Hebrew has no separate numbers, only the letters. Each letter therefore has two functions: to combine with others to form words and to demarcate a numerical value.

For example, the Hebrew word for light is *Or.* It is comprised of three letters: *aleph, vov,* and *reish.* The first Hebrew letter—*Aleph*—has the numerical value of one. The *vov* has the numerical value of six and the *reish* of two hundred. Thus the Hebrew word for light—*Or*—has the total value of two hundred and seven.

Kabbalists have long taught that the correspondences between words with the same numerical values are quite significant. They are even seen to be interchangeable, in the sense that a mathematician would regard numbers. For instance, another Hebrew word with the total value of two hundred and seven is "mystery". Therefore, Kabbalists see a certain cosmic relationship between "light" and "mystery" of the universe.

Jewish mystics teach that God built into the Hebrew language precisely this sort of celestial code. We can certainly speak Hebrew in an everyday way; but a supernal significance is seen to comprise each of its letters. For this is the language in which the Bible was originally written. To Kabbalists, it is no ordinary language at all.

For millennia, Jewish mystics have indeed declared that each Hebrew letter communicates three separate branches of meaning. The first is the letter's numerical value. The second is its sound—and this is very important in Kabbalistic practice. And the third is its shape. All three are vital to deciphering the code in which the Bible is written.

The sound of the Hebrew letter is quite significant, because it establishes the basis for certain forms of mantra-like meditation. In this sense, too, the reference in Genesis 1 to "And God said" is seen to suggest the incredible power inherent in human speech when properly focused through meditation.

The shape of the letter is likewise vital, because it contains visually coded information—like a mandala. A mandala is the Eastern term for an image that serves as the focal point for meditation. By gazing at the image, we can achieve higher states of consciousness. These three areas of meaning come up again and again in the Kabbalistic approach to the Bible. They are in fact essential to its mystical interpretation.

Opening Line of Genesis

Let us turn now to the text of the Bible and examine its very famous first line: "In the beginning, God created heaven and earth." As we shall see, Kabbalists insist that a more accurate and meaningful translation from the Hebrew should read: "In the beginning, X created God *et* the heaven and *et* the earth." That is, the English translation almost invariably offers a very misleading and considerably over-simplified version. (The use of *et* as a synonym for the Hebrew alphabet will be discussed further on.)

For example, a fundamental Kabbalistic work—the *Tikkuney Zohar*—devotes an entire book to these first words. Jewish mystics approach the words as though they are the clothes that surround a being within them. We must therefore seek the soul or message inside the outer cloak of the words.

Why does the Bible begin with the letter *Beth*? This is the first question Kabbalists ask. It is a particularly relevant question because *Beth* is not the first Hebrew letter but the second. Many explanations are traditionally provided. One explanation is that the Bible is not really describing the absolute beginning—that to begin the Bible with the second letter is a clue or signal that the account has omitted reference to that which came before.

A second explanation focuses on the shape of the letter *Beth*. Kabbalists teach that the shape of every letter is meaningful and significant. The *Beth* is open in only one direction—this suggests that time and events in our universe flow only one way. Also, the *Beth* has a little tail that points back like a trail; this tail suggests that something lies back there.

Third, the *Beth* is prefixed in Hebrew to certain words to impart a specific meaning: it signifies the notion of either "in" or "with". Thus, the Bible's opening phrase can mean "In the Beginning" or "With the beginning". Kabbalists view both interpretations as valid and feel that both interpretations teach us something about the universe. The seeming ambiguities of the Hebrew are seen to reflect the subtleties of existence itself. This is vitally important in the Kabbalistic system; the Bible's apparent ambiguities are not a "problem" but a way to teach us many truths in a very condensed manner.

Within this word which is typically translated as "In the beginning" lies another, root word. This root word—*reshit*—actually has three different meanings: beginning, head, and wisdom or *chokmah*. *Chokmah* has its own specifically mystical connotations. So we can begin to see the great complexity by which the Bible is written when it is considered from the Kabbalistic perspective!

Let us look briefly at the second word now. *Bara* can denote "created", but is can also denote "healed". In other words, we can say, "In the beginning, God created" or "In wisdom, God created" or "With the beginning, God created" or "In the beginning, God healed (the heaven and the earth)" or "With the beginning, God healed (the heaven and the earth." To Kabbalists, all of these declarations are valid and coherent; perhaps the true purpose of this sentence is not to tell us about the beginning of time but to relate a cosmic healing that occurred at some unimaginable moment.

We can also say, "In the head, God created (the heaven and the earth)." This might connote that God created "with His head" this universe. Indeed, there is an entire interpretation of this first chapter of Genesis that insists that everything is described on a spiritual and transcendent level—a level of God's thought. This interpretation says that the account of physical creation doesn't begin until the second chapter of Genesis, for many discrepancies seem to exist between the first two chapters. It is almost as if two different narratives are offered.

We can further read the text in the following ways:

1) "With the head, God created";
2) "Using His head, God created";
3) "In the head, God healed";
4) "With the head, God healed";
5) "In wisdom, God created";
6) "With wisdom, God created";
7) "In wisdom, God healed";
8) "With wisdom, God healed."

These eight translations—coupled with the earlier four—produce a total of twelve: an important Kabbalistic number. There are twelve tribes of Israel, twelve signs of the Zodiac.

Thus, the first two words of the Bible generate twelve different ways of reading—and all are legitimate. Then a Kabbalist moves on to the phrase "the heaven and the earth". We can now begin to glimpse the complex ramifications and permutations manifested in every line of the Bible. We can also see the truly abitrary nature of the English translations; most say simply, "In the beginning, God created. . ." A few Aramaic translations say, "With wisdom, God created. . ." But other, Kabbalistic translations certainly exist.

Another crucial point is that without knowledge of the subtleties of the Hebrew language, we would never even realize that these other translations are possible. We could meditate for days on the typical English version and never know that many other meanings exist in the text. Only through comprehension of the Hebrew Bible can we really begin to know it.

Let us look at the third word of the Bible—*Elokim*, usually translated as "God". Kabbalists believe that only the Hebrew word *Ain Sof* connotes "God", so that *Elokim* must refer to something else. This is one problem with the modern translation. Another problem is that the Hebrew ending is a plural one; *Elokim* is a plural word. Jewish mystics teach that it means neither "God" nor "gods", but rather that it is a particular *sefira*—a name of God—and a force of creation. It comprises five letters and this too is of significance.

Elokim is one of the ten *sefiroth*. But it also represents all the *sefiroth*, because they can be grouped into five sets of two. These five groups are known as *partzufim* from the Greek word *partzuf* meaning "persona". Therefore, each of the five letters of the word *Elokim* refers to one of the groups of two *sefiroth*.

For Kabbalists, then, *Elokim* is one of the ten *sefiroth* but at the same time it encompasses all the others. This is why *Elokim* because of its five letters is often a shorthand way of discussing all the *sefiroth* together. This certainly can become confusing—that there are ten which become five in the *partzufim*. Thus, another way to read the opening phrase of the Bible is, "In the beginning, the *sefiroth* created the heaven and the earth."

If you now look at the Hebrew, you see a more literal translation. Let us assume that *Bereshis* means "In the beginning" and *bara* means "created". This indicates that, "in the beginning created God". If we insert the word "was"—and we will come back to the justification for that interpolation—the phrase reads, "In the beginning was created God." This is how Kabbalists understand the text—that in the beginning God created Himself.

By this interpretation, Jewish mystics teach that *Ain Sof* intended to create a universe. To accomplish this, the *sefiroth* were created. Therefore, the Bible is really relating that in the beginning were the *sefiroth* and the alphabet of the heaven and the alphabet of the earth. The first thing that was created was *Elokim* and then after that were created other things.

Therefore, by inserting the word "was" in this verse, we can understand a difficult passage in a new and meaningful way; this is because a word seemed to be missing and "was" can be inserted to make sense out of the passage. Now, by substituting *Ain Sof* for "was", the verse finally reads, "In the beginning, *Ain Sof* created the *et* of the heaven and the *et* of the earth."

Returning, then, to the Bible, we can now read the opening phrase as, "In the beginning, the *sefiroth* created the heaven and the earth." That is yet another way to read the passage. There is another place in the Bible where the same situation occurs: Exodus 24:1. The English translation relates, "God said to Moses, 'Go up to God along with Aaron, Nadav and Avihu, and seventy of the elders of Israel.' " But the Hebrew actually says, "And to Moses said, 'Come up. . .' " This is very puzzling, for how do we make sense of "And to Moses said?" Obviously there seems to be a word missing. The English translation inserts the word "God", but there is no intervening word in the Hebrew Bible.

Kabbalists interpret this mystery as offering us a hint of the concept of *Ain Sof*. As was true for the verse in Genesis, a word has been omitted and it is seen to reflect *Ain Sof*. So, "To Moses *Ain Sof* said" is what we can substitute for the Hebrew version. This tells us immediately that Moses had achieved such a lofty level of prophecy that he could communicate directly with *Ain Sof*, beyond the realm of the *sefiroth*. This is the only place in the Bible that such a prophetic state is suggested, for it is precisely at this point in the Biblical narrative—right after the giving of the Ten Commandments— that Moses had to cover himself with a veil because his face was shining so brightly.

It is important to recognize that there are multiple levels at which the Bible can be understood. On the simplest level, it would certainly be correct to say that "God created the heaven and the earth." When we speak on a deeper level, we do not invalidate the simpler ones; rather, we elaborate subtleties not readily apparent. Each way of approaching the text also gives us a different type of insight. On one level, then, we can say, "God created the heaven and the earth." Or, "In the beginning, God created the heaven and the earth." On another level, we can also state, "In the beginning, God was created" or "In the beginning, Elokim was created," which is the Kabbalistic way of reading this line. But Kabbalists would not read the line in exclusion to "In the beginning, God created the heaven and the earth," but as an addition to that line. Thus, they are adding a new dimension rather than denigrating the old one.

Remember, there are twelve different ways to look at the first two words of the Bible—and we have not even reached the word "God" yet. It is vital to understand, though, that each of these ways lends some section of the truth. The truth is so complex that it could not possibly be contained in any one thing; the Bible's method of writing in such a way as to convey all these permutations imparts more meaning to the narrative.

THE GOD OF THE BIBLE

If we adopt the Jewish mystical perspective that *Ain Sof* created *Elokim*, then the entire Bible becomes much easier to understand. We can comprehend how *Elokim* becomes angry and exhibits all the other human attributes; we can comprehend too why different names of this permutation of *Elokim* are used. Remember, *Elokim* is *not* God.

At the same time, we must understand that the existence of *Elokim* is the means by which human individuals can communicate with *Ain Sof*. But *Elokim* is not to be mistaken for God. This Kabbalistic teaching sheds light on the Second Commandment, "You shall have no other gods before me." Note that the verse does not say, "There are no other gods but me." It says, "You shall have no other gods before me."

Kabbalists interpret this verse to indicate that these other gods—derived from the *sefiroth*—are indeed real; they are godlike. But humans are not to worship them or pray to them or give homage to them; the *sefiroth* are only intermediaries to the *Ain Sof*. Within Judaism, the *sefiroth* are valued as part of the system of divine communication between us and the *Ain Sof*, but they are never to be worshipped as independent entities.

To summarize, there are two indirect biblical allusions to God; both occur in places where a word is left out. Other than these omissions—which could be filled in by the word meaning "God"—there is no mention of "God" anywhere in the Bible. Only the ten *sefiroth* are mentioned.

It is interesting to note that English uses only one word/ name to refer to "God", but that Hebrew has these many names. This linguistic phenomenon is similar to the popular analogy pertaining to the Eskimo language and its varied expressions for "snow". In English we have only one word— "snow". But the Eskimos have twenty different words that mean "snow". This is because the different nuances of snow are so crucial to their daily lives. Thus, they might say to a non-Eskimo, "What kind of snow are you talking about? Is it wet snow or hard-packed snow?" Their linguistic structure undoubtedly affects many aspects of their lives,too, from their type of clothing to their mode of hunting.

Analogously, the English language contains this one word —"God"—but the Bible sets forth ten different words, each one referring to a particular manifestation of the primal forces of Creation. These are known as the *sefiroth*.

The Alphabet of Creation

The first and last Hebrew letters when placed together form a word—*Et*—which is often translated into English as "the". Thus, some Biblical translations state, "In the beginning, God created the heaven and the earth." But note that a literal translation from the Hebrew reads as follows, "In the beginning, God created *et* the heaven and *et* the earth." Kabbalistically, because the word *et* is comprised of the first and last letters, it has been viewed as a synonym for the Hebrew alphabet itself. Therefore, we can translate this opening sentence as, "In the beginning, God created the alphabet of the heaven and the alphabet of the earth."

What does this "alphabet" refer to? In modern terms, the "alphabet" is the secret genetic code embedded in the Hebrew words of the Bible. For example, it is now theoretically possible for a genetic scientist to look at the chemical symbols that describe some genetic material and to conclude, "This is the formula for a dog. It is a German shepherd with blue eyes and a brown tail." Or, the scientist might examine the chemical symbols describing some other genetic material and comment, "This is the formula for an elephant. It is female and blind in one eye." Or, the scientist might examine still other genetic material and observe, "This is the formula for a very strange beast. It is half rabbit and half giraffe." The point is that all the information about the particular animal is encoded within its genes.

Kabbalists have for millennia viewed the Hebrew language in a very similar manner. That is, each Hebrew word—with its particular combination of letters—is seen as a genetic-like code for the word. For example, take the Hebrew word for "dog". By truly understanding the interrelation of the three letters of this word, Kabbalists insist, we know the very essence of a dog's nature—its "dogginess".

The Hebrew term et, therefore, is the divine alphabet— the genetic-like structure for everything in the universe. In the beginning, then, was created the et and once the et was created all else occurred with "And God said". Kabbalists speak of the first "And God said" that preceded "In the beginning". However, they view this divine speech as akin to silence; for the et had not yet been created.

Jewish mystics note that the phrase "And God said" occurs in Genesis a specific number of times. That total number is very important and each particular mention of this phrase is also important, signifying another force of creation. Also, they stress that creation is not something that simply happened in the distant past but rather it is a celestial process occurring at every instant in the cosmos. Thus, the seemingly repetitive statements, "And God said" are viewed as keys to the ongoing process of creation.

Kabbalists further interpret the phrase "And God said" as a message that speech is the vehicle of creation. They infer from this section of the Bible that speech is something divine and godlike, possessing a generative power of its own. We are taught, therefore, that humans are the only animals on the planet that actually speak. Other species certainly communicate in the sense that an alarm bell is a communication to its listeners. But an alarm bell is not speech and the other species do not use speech. The whole question of what differentiates speech from mere sound is treated very thoroughly in the Jewish esoteric tradition.

On this subject, there is the intriguing concept of the *Golem*. Kabbalists teach that a *Golem* is a human-like form—an android in modern terms—which can work and perform various tasks. According to Jewish mystics, humans can create *Golems* by performing certain specific meditative rituals involving the pronunciation of various Hebrew words. Jewish history records through quite reliable sages the creation of such beings. We mention the *Golems* here because the Kabbalah declares that they cannot speak; this lack is what ultimately distinguishes them from humans. Thus, the power to use speech is seen as a very important feature of our earthly existence.

Manipulating the Forces of Creation

Today, nearly everyone is familiar with the topic of genetic research. It is quite controversial and religious leaders of all faiths have offered their opinions on it. Scientifically, we have arrived at the point where we can create new life forms. In doing this, we can create substances which may prove very beneficial to humans. Yet, this same process can unleash very destructive forms; for example, scientists might accidentally create a new virus or a new bacteria, causing a disease for which there is no cure and whole populations might die. Another black plague might happen from this research. Clearly, great dangers potentially exist: someone might choose to use genetic research in a malicious way; perhaps more likely, uncontrolled and virulent life forms might accidentally be created. And clearly, too, genetic research might be a wonderful boon for humankind.

Should we establish a legal body empowered to make decisions about genetic research? Who should have access to such research? Who should conduct it? How should such a legal body be constituted? These are all very important and controversial questions for us today.

For Kabbalists in ancient times, precisely the same sorts of questions loomed. As mentioned, they believed that intimate knowledge of the Bible allowed an individual to actually create new life forms. Understanding of the forces represented by the Hebrew letters, coupled with the ability to combine the letters properly, was seen to enable one to manipulate the very forces of creation in our universe. Indeed, the first chapter of Genesis was regarded as containing sufficient information for any individual to create new forms. From this perspective, therefore, the issue of permitting or denying access to the Kabbalah was a very real and serious one for early Jewish mystics. The legend of the *Golem* certainly relates to this topic. According to Kabbalists, the *Golem* was not created through the modern process of cloning, but from a different process. The Kabbalah teaches that various *Golems* have been created over the centuries. Mystical texts exist that purport to describe how to create a *Golem* through specific meditative techniques. The Bible itself offers at least one reference to such beings; later Kabbalistic texts provided much more detailed information, but usually in a kind of code.

The next questions to arise concern basic Kabbalistic metaphysics. What is God's relation to our universe and other realms that may exist? In what ways do we each relate to God? It is to such intriguing topics that we now turn.

CHAPTER FOUR

Sacred Metaphysics

THE REALM OF BETH

As we have already seen, the Bible begins with the letter *Beth*, the second—not the first—letter in the Hebrew alphabet, and we have examined two time-honored Kabbalistic explanations for this situation. But there is a third to consider. This teaching affirms that ultimately everything in the universe comprises a fundamental oneness. As pointed out before, superficially, at least, a piece of excrement and a diamond are very, very different. But once we start to reach their atomic and then subatomic makeup, we find that the two substances are incredibly alike: there is virtually no difference between them. This state of being is known as the realm of *Aleph*, where all is an undifferentiated wholeness.

But the Kabbalah goes on to affirm too that our existence pertains to the realm of *Beth*, where there is separation. The reality of our lives is that the excrement and the diamond are different. From the vantage point of *Aleph*, we are all a Unity; but from our place in the realm of *Beth*, separateness is quite real. This notion can be seen as a third distinct message emanating from the fact that *Beth*, not *Aleph*, is the opening letter of the Bible.

THE SECOND VERSE OF GENESIS

Let us directly examine the second sentence of Genesis. It declares, "The earth was without form..." In Hebrew, this sentence is phrased quite interestingly, for the first part is in the past tense and the next set of parts is in the present tense. Thus, this sentence actually contains three parts. The first is that "The earth was void and empty"; this is described using the past tense. The second is that "darkness is on the face of the deep"; this is described using the present tense. The third is that "God's spirit is moving on the water"; this, too, is written in the present tense.

For this reason, Kabbalists have interpreted the passage to signify that the second sentence of Genesis refers to something that preceded in time the reference of the first sentence. In other words, the first sentence of Genesis provides a general view of Creation; then the second sentence returns to the specifics of what happened before the description of the first sentence. Remember, the Bible begins with the second letter, *Beth*. Kabbalists insist that there was an entire process that occurred in the realm of *Aleph*—not directly mentioned at all in the Bible. A clue to this situation is that the second sentence of Genesis begins in the past tense and speaks of what was before; only then does it utilize the present tense.

The second sentence also offers more information about the specifics for meditation. In English, the sentence reads, "The earth was without form and empty, with darkness on the face of the depth, but God's spirit moved on the water's surface." The English words "was without form and empty", however, are quite a loose translation of the Hebrew. The truth is that no one really knows what the Hebrew words *tohu* and *bohu* mean. They are very strange words and occur nowhere else in the Bible.

Tohu is traditionally related to the concept of "confusion". *Bohu* is comprised of two units: *bo* (meaning "in it") and *hu* (meaning "he"). Thus, *bohu* seems to signify "he is in it", or something to that effect. This connotation is quite different— almost opposite, in fact—from the typical English translation of "empty". The Hebrew connotes that "something" was certainly there, but the nature of that "something" is rather enigmatic. We can best translate the passage as saying, "The earth was without *tohu* and *bohu* with darkness on the face of the deep. . ." The English words "form and empty" are thus only two of many possible interpretations for these cryptic Hebrew terms.

Next, the Bible states, "with darkness on the face of the deep". If we examine the entire sentence closely, we now can see that it represents a description for the process of meditation. The first stage of meditation is that of *tohu*—confusion—where a lot of confused things occur. We experience whirring images, jumbled thoughts rushing through our minds. The second state of meditation occurs when we begin to attain glimpses of information coming through. The information is not yet very clear, but "something is there". We are still in a state of consciousness in which confusion reigns, but we now have the awareness that "something is there".

The third stage of meditation is when we attempt to focus on what is there. We enter into the "darkness"—the nothingness—because we have already penetrated beyond all the reverie whirling about in our mind. We have arrived at a much deeper state of consciousness. The fourth stage of meditation is what we reach when we go beyond that deep place of darkness: God's spirit.

From this perspective, we can see that the Bible's narrative of Creation is not meant to tell history or cosmology, but to serve as a spiritual handbook. We are being given information as to what to expect as we embark on the meditative process, as well as to know which step we are on. This section precedes the first sentence. Therefore, we begin meditation by focusing on the *Shin* and *Mem*; then, as we move on to the second sentence, we start our meditation on light. In this way, the Bible unfolds sentence by sentence as a practical manual for achieving loftier consciousness.

Now we come to a very intriguing and important section of Genesis: the reference to "darkness". It is crucial to note that "darkness" is mentioned before "light" in the account of Creation. The first sentence is, "In the beginning, God created the heaven and the earth." The second sentence is, "The earth was without form and empty, with darkness on the face of the deep, but God's spirit moved on the water." And the third sentence contains the first reference to "light".

What does this teach us? The Kabbalah offers many, many interpretations on this point. One notion certainly is that in order for us to appreciate light, darkness must exist. If there was only light and no darkness, we could never develop an appreciation for light. This is a simple psychological truth, not a mystical conception. A mystical interpretation, though, is this: if the light did not come after the darkness, then we would never be able to bring light out of darkness. To apply this principle to our own lives, we sometimes feel that we are surrounded by darkness. But this passage emphasizes that we can always bring light to the dark places of our existence; darkness can always lead to light. This is another message built into the text of Genesis.

The Lineage of the Messiah

Behind Kabbalistic metaphysics lies even a deeper message. This is the notion that the Messiah—literally, "the annointed one"—will come from darkness. He will arise from the lowest, most base elements of humanity. This is an interesting idea and derives partly from the view that the Messiah will have to attract all people; he will have to reach the lowest and most base individuals among us, not just the exalted ones. Thus, the Messiah's roots will come from darkness, from the most base places.

We all know that the Messiah will arise from the House of David. No one else is named. The Messiah will come solely from the House of David, we are long told with the clear implication that there is something very special about this lineage. This is a very ancient concept within Judaism. For instance, the early Christians were very concerned with demonstrating that Jesus was a descendant of the House of David. Since the Bible explicitly stated that the Messiah would be an offspring of King David, the New Testament sought to document that Jesus' roots went back to David. It gives us the account that Jesus was born and raised in Bethlehem, just as David was.

King David was of course very popular, much beloved in

the Jewish nation. He was a very righteous, holy man. But when we trace his family roots, where did he come from? The Bible tells us clearly. First, David was a descendant of Ruth on one side and of Judah on the other. But where did Ruth come from? She was a descendant of Lot. But which descendant of Lot? The Bible relates an interesting story about the towns of Sodom and Gemorrah that God destroyed. Lot and his family were the only ones who escaped alive from the decimation; after it, he engaged in incest with his two daughters. It is this incestuous relationship that gave rise to the maternal side of David through Ruth.

What about David's paternal side? Another incestuous relationship was involved. It occurred between Judah and his daughter-in-law. Their union gave birth to Peretz, who became a paternal ancestor of David. The Bible narrates closely this important episode. In those times there was a Jewish law that if a husband died before producing any children, then his brother was obligated to marry the dead man's wife, so that the deceased's lineage would continue. What happened is that one of Judah's sons married a woman named Tamar and died before they produced any children. Thus, Judah instructed his second son to marry the widow; but the second son also died. Thereupon, Judah told Tamar that his third son was still quite young and that she should wait at her parents' home for a few years before marrying him. Tamar did so, but Judah forgot all about her and never instructed his third son to prepare to marry her.

Tamar then decided to take matters into her own hands, so to speak. She disguised herself as a prostitute and placed herself by the road in order to seduce Judah and produce a child through their union. Tamar's plan worked. Before Judah took his leave from her, though, she made sure he gave her some of his belongings as her "payment". Tamar became pregnant. Judah, never suspecting that he had been seduced by Tamar, was enraged to learn that she had become pregnant while still a widow. He ordered that she be killed as punishment. Just as Judah's countrymen prepared to kill her, she suddenly produced his belongings and declared, "My baby's father is the owner of these garments." At that moment Judah realized what had happened and took responsibility for his child-to-be. That child was Peretz, who became a paternal ancestor of David.

David's lineage is therefore quite fascinating. On one side, Lot and his daughter; on the other side, Peretz. We can again see the notion that the light will spring from darkness and that the brilliant light of the Messiah will arise from the darkness of human sexual intrigue. In this context, Saul, the first King of Israel, had truly impeccable family credentials. He really came from a distinguished family and there was nothing amiss in his lineage. And yet it was David, the second King of Israel, who came from the worst of lineages and was granted the honor of serving as the ancestor of the Messiah. There are other biblical tales that record this same phenomenon: that something goes wrong with the first born or the first chosen, and then the second one must carry out the mission. For example, Moses was not the first born son and yet he became the leader.

Our whole point in this discussion is that light must spring from darkness. In the ultimate salvation or ultimate light, the darkest places will have to be reached and transformed. Only one who is steeped in that darkness—in one way or another—will have the strength and empathy to effect the transformation. The Kabbalah even teaches the seemingly unfair notion that one who has truly sinned and repented is on a higher spiritual level than one who has never sinned and done only righteous things. This is a very clear concept within Judaism.

AIN SOF AND CREATION

Now let us return to the theme of light originating from darkness. It is central to the Kabbalistic view of how the universe was created. If *Ain Sof* was to create the cosmos, where could He have accomplished this? There was only *Ain Sof* at that time. We have already made use of the analogy to the sun and our planet. We cannot travel too close to the sun or we will be evaporated. Rather, we must establish some basic distance before we can coexist with it. We must be so many millions of miles away or we would all evaporate. Now, how far can we get from God in order to exist as separate points of being? Is there enough distance that something can get from *Ain Sof*, so that it will not be extinguished by His radiance? Where can lowly matter exist in order to have sufficient distance from that unimaginable power?

The Kabbalistic answer is that God had to make a space for the universe to exist and not be extinguished by His radiance. There was *Ain Sof* and there was a "light" of *Ain Sof* called *Ain Sof-Ohr* that emanated all around. The only way to create a cosmos was therefore to make a void—an absence of light, a vacuum—so that something other than *Ain Sof* could exist. *Ain Sof* had to withdraw some of His radiance to allow for differentiation and identity. Therefore, a darkness or void was created before the light of our universe. This is because nothing can exist in God's presence unless God "hides" or "removes" Himself to some degree; if God does not do so, then there would be only God.

Kabbalists have historically provided a variety of diagrams to make this metaphysical abstraction more clear. Imagine that this space is black. Out there, it is all white—all the light of *Ain Sof*—and within it, a black hole or a space of darkness was created. Within the space, a line of light emanated outward to a central dot. Essentially, Kabbalists say that God effected a "vacated space"—He contracted part of Himself—in order for our universe to come into being. Without that contraction, there could have been no separate creation.

Creation implies duality. So, the Bible relates, "In the beginning, God created. . ." These five words tell us a great deal. Creation means duality. But the Hebrew word *Elokim* (a Name of God) indicates plurality. As we have seen, *Elokim* is Kabbalistically viewed to encompass the five *partzufim*. Thus, we are describing duality and plurality in the very first sentence of the Bible. Just keep in mind the analogy that if a room were now flooded with light and one wished to develop a photograph, one would have to create a dark space in which to do it. Thus, essentially, there had to be this darkness built into the very design of Creation.

THE NATURE OF EVIL

We come next to another, very intriguing concept about darkness, and that is its relation to evil. Kabbalists certainly equate darkness with evil. Therefore, from this perspective, God inserted evil into the very fabric of the cosmos; before there was even good, evil existed in our universe. The reason for this is that the vacated space constituted the absence of *Ain Sof* or God—and by definition, the absence of God is evil. Kabbalists almost define good and evil spatially—in their distance from God. They are not implying, of course, that there is an actual physical space out there, but that closeness to God is good and distance is evil. The closer we draw to God, the more good; the further we move from Him, the more evil. So remember: evil is not defined as "badness" but in terms of distance from God. From the beginning, then, evil or the distance from God existed with our universe.

Why did God do things this way? It is not really possible to attempt to psychoanalyze God, but we can certainly grapple with the idea that He could have effected Creation in other ways; He could have chosen any way He wished. Therefore, if God carried out Creation in this particular way, He must have done so for reasons that relate to the entire blueprint of our system. What, then, might be the reason or justification for building evil into the very fabric of our cosmos? What could possibly be the function of evil and its preeminent place in Creation?

The Kabbalah teaches that the creation of evil was perhaps the greatest gift that God gave man. Adepts have long taught that the myriad realms that exist all do so to serve man; therefore, evil must exist for this same purpose. How does evil help us? The answer lies in the concept of human free will. For God wanted man not to be a robot-like being—a programmed machine—but something far, far greater and more godlike. He had to make man totally free—free to defy God, to not listen to Him. If man had been created only able to obey God, he would have lacked freedom and been much less godlike. Of course, the ability to defy God immediately implies the possibility of evil because evil, by definition, represents a going away from God.

Thus, to set the stage for human free will, evil had to exist from the very beginning. For if it did not exist, then whatever came afterwards would not be free. Again, evil means the ability to defy or resist God. Now, there are very few parents who can give their children the kind of freedom that God gave us. So, in a sense, it must involve a great love to be able to make another being completely independent from you. We all know this from our relationships with one another; too often we want people to become dependent on us, to become extensions of ourselves. God's relationship to humanity constitutes a model, in a way, for our relation with our children and with one another.

The Kabbalistic conception of God is really quite different from the simplistic notion that our failings anger Him. For if that were true, then we would actually control God—be able to make Him happy or sad, angry or calm. God remains unchanged by what we do. In a sense, God is the ideal parent, the ideal therapist. He is there. Whatever is, is. The Bible clearly elucidates this principle when God says, "I am God. I am unchangeable."

However, to effect a communication system between God and man, *Ain Sof* or God created a set of ten forces—*Sefiroth*—that went on to create this universe. *Ain Sof* did not directly conduct Creation, but did so indirectly through the *Sefiroth*. These forces possess certain characteristics, including what we would call emotional components. We are patterned on these forces; therefore, our psychology, mode of thinking, and logic are patterned on the *Sefiroth*. Our qualities of anger and revenge, then, are patterned on the ten forces, but God is many steps above them. God remains beyond any attributes.

REWARD, PUNISHMENT AND THE DIVINE FEEDBACK LOOP

A key Kabbalistic premise is that a divine feedback loop exists between each of us and the ten forces. From the traditional Jewish viewpoint, man is the center of Creation; therefore, there is something very special about man that differentiates him from every other animate or inanimate substance in the universe. This is the reality that only man is connected with a feedback loop to these recondite forces. Not even angels are endowed with this capacity.

What does this situation mean? Quite simply that man's action can actually influence or change the basic forces of Creation. Remember, the Kabbalah teaches that Creation continues anew at every instant; we therefore interact with the forces that at this very moment sustain the entire universe. This means that the forces respond to what we do. It will appear to us that they respond in a human manner; thus, they may seem angered at times by our actions. But they are not *Ain Sof* and this point must be repeated throughout this book. The *Sefiroth* are not really angry, but they might seem that way from our limited perspective; we are mirror images of the *Sefiroth*.

If man possesses some measure of free will, then so do the *Sefiroth*. They are the blueprint, in a sense, for man. But God Himself is beyond such concerns. God formed the communication system that constitutes the *Sefiroth*; God put evil into the system for free will to exist. That is why evil or darkness is mentioned so early in the Bible.

The Kabbalah teaches that there is really no such thing as divine punishment and reward *per se*. Nobody is really punished or rewarded; rather, there are consequences for every thing that we do, say, or think. *Ain Sof* says, "I have created the universe and there are certain laws—spiritual as well as physical—by which it functions. I am going to give you the laws in a book—the Torah. If you understand the laws, then you can make the most out of what you have. But if you defy the laws, then you will suffer the consequences of that defiance."

An analogy to this notion is the child who puts his hand on a hot stove or the adult who sticks his hand in a fire. Both are going to get burned and it will hurt. The child might say, "The fire punished me" or "The fire got angry at me," but the adult certainly would not. The adult clearly understands that the fire did not purposely hurt him or her, that the pain comes from the nature of human flesh and of fire. There is no notion of good or bad in this context; it is simply the way things are in our corner of the universe. The Torah therefore comes to say: these are the spiritual laws that describe the nature of things. If one performs in certain ways, one will experience certain results. If one behaves in other ways, then one will experience quite different consequences. God does not angrily "punish" nor happily "reward" us any more than the fire emotionally responds to our actions. This is an important point to ponder. The Torah is intended to convey in complete detail all the information pertinent to human behavior and its spiritual consequences. But nobody is standing somewhere up in the sky ready to club us if we err. In this sense, not even the *Sefiroth* can become angry with man; such a notion is only man's anthropomorphic explanation — as a child would say, "The fire got angry and punished me."

A further point must be made. When the Bible narrates, "I am God. I am unchangeable," it is not really *Ain Sof* that is speaking. However, the prophet is nevertheless receiving divine information from the *Sefiroth*. *Ain Sof* uses the *Sefiroth* as a method of communication to man. The prophet is then able to decode the information and say, "I heard about *Ain Sof* that this is what *Ain Sof* is saying." He may have heard about it through the *Sefirah* of Elohim or El Shaddai, but the information concerned *Ain Sof*.

ANGELS

The Kabbalah teaches that one of the main distinguishing features between a man and an angel is that only man has free will. Angels are beings that occupy a much higher spiritual level than man; they are much closer to God. But angels are like robots, in a sense, for they are obliged or "programmed" to follow God always. They do not possess the capacity to defy God and, hence, have no real choice in their actions.

The angel is essentially a servant of God; the Hebrew word for "angel", spelled in another way, also signifies "messenger". The angel therefore can be conceptualized as a messenger. It is assigned to carry out certain functions that God directs. God says, "Do this", and the angel will go and do it. So, despite the lofty plane of the angel's existence, it is fixed forever on its particular "rung" on the heavenly ladder. In contrast, man can ultimately come closer to God than can any angel because man possesses free will. We are not fixed in our development. By following the path of the Torah and the Kabbalah, each of us can attain levels higher than angels. This potential lies within everyone.

Satan: God's Loyal Servant

In the context of Kabbalistic concepts about evil, it is helpful to focus briefly on the intriguing topic of the devil. How does the devil fit into the metaphysical system around us and what is his function? Be aware that Judaism has historically dealt quite specifically with this subject. Indeed, the devil—Satan—is mentioned directly in the Bible. Look at the Book of Job. The devil is very much a part of classic Jewish theology.

What, then, is the Jewish devil? The Jewish conception of Satan is quite unlike its counterpart in historical Christianity. According to Judaism, Satan is a very faithful servant of God—one of His most faithful servants. Since God has created evil, the realm of evil belongs to Satan. But this realm is really a gift to man—insuring his capacity of free will—and so Satan has a very important task to perform. It is his mission to do precisely what God wants him to do, for the Kabbalah teaches that nothing is more powerful than *Ain Sof.*

To explain more clearly Satan's role in human life Kabbalists have long told the following story. Adepts relate that there was once a king who ruled over a vast kingdom. The king had a son. One day, the king began to think of the future and of the time when his son would be the next king. And the king wondered whether his son was actually suited for this position. Was he mature enough? Could he handle the responsibilities? Did he possess the necessary inner resources? The king decided to find out. He wanted to test his son to see whether he could indeed be a powerful and just ruler.

The king therefore called his son in and said to him, "As prince of the kingdom, you will now be given a great deal of authority to exercise. I am going to give you plenty of wealth and power; you will be able to do many things. As a matter of fact, you have my blessing to do almost anything you want in the kingdom. But there is one thing I want you *not* to do. If you will just avoid this one thing, everything else will be yours and you will have all of my blessings. The one thing I want you not to do is this: you must never engage in any kind of premarital sex. Other than this, you can have anything in my kingdom and you have the power now to do what you want." The son agreed; he replied, "Fine. I accept the conditions." No sooner did he leave than the king called in the most beautiful, seductive prostitute in his entire kingdom. The king said to her, "I will give you ten million dollars in gold if you can get my son into bed with you. Use all of your charms; do anything you wish to seduce him. If you succeed, this tremendous reward will be yours."

So off the prostitute went to find the king's son. The stage was now set; the players were the king, his son, and the prostitute. The question that Jewish mystics have for millennia asked is: is not the prostitute simply doing the king's bidding. Can we say that she is evil or even bad? She is simply doing precisely what the king requested of her.

Now, keep this story in mind as we return to the issue of the Jewish devil. Kabbalists compare the king to God and the son to humanity. The prostitute was not even really a prostitute but a very loyal subject of the king who agreed to play the part. She was really an extremely moral, loyal woman—and this view is exactly how Kabbalists regard the devil. He is a very loyal servant of God, being sent on a mission involving humanity.

In terms of our analogy, the prostitute is certainly trying her very best to carry out the king's request. She may be secretly hoping that the son will resist her wiles, but she will use every charm she possesses to seduce him. In the same way, the devil is seen as a very loyal servant of God who is bound by God's word. The devil does only what God bids and is there to set the stage to allow for man's free will. In Judaism, then, the devil is not regarded as a malevolent or evil entity challenging God's rule. Indeed, the Talmud says quite clearly, "Do as the devil does but not as the devil says." This is because the devil does only what God asks. Judaism has many allusions to this concept: that the devil is an entity very close to God and that the function of evil is to ensure human free will. Kabbalists teach that our relation to evil fundamentally changed when Adam and Eve ate the forbidden fruit in the Garden of Eden. Until that moment evil existed but it was outside of man. With the eating of the forbidden fruit, evil actually became incorporated into the human soul or psyche. Ever since that time evil has existed within us; it has been part of our nature as earthly creatures.

REACHING GOD THROUGH EVIL

There is one more point to consider about evil from a Kabbalistic perspective. It is the notion that since evil is a creation of God, there is a path to God through evil; one can reach God through evil. However, the Kabbalah insists that this is one of the forbidden paths; these paths work but are not meant for human beings. For example, the ancient *Sefer Yetzirah* ("Book of Creation") identifies the different, possible paths to God represented by the *Sefiroth*. One of these is the path of evil, and it is forbidden.

What is the consequence of embarking on a forbidden path? Adolf Hitler and the Nazi Party offer a vivid example of an involvement with the path of evil. Recent scholars have documented quite thoroughly the Nazis' interest in black magic and the occult. Indeed, Hitler had to make a choice early in his career: to further his spiritual development through the path of righteousness or the path of evil. Hitler possessed almost enough power to rule the world. There were many attempts on his life—well-conceived plots—and each one failed. It was almost as if some force was intervening to allow him to go on and achieve his desired end. At one point, Hitler began to use psychedelic drugs as a means to effect very rapid inner development that he would need later in his rule as *Der Fuhrer*. He had expert teachers who saw in him a raw potential, and they helped guide his development until he could begin to use his inner power. (Some believe that he managed to get hold of the spear which pierced Jesus on the cross; this spear has long been associated with black magical power.)

The evidence is strong that Hitler's mentors—and the Nazi Party's inner core—were all quite involved with black magic, the path of evil or darkness. Many of the atrocities they carried out were actually ritualistic acts of murder for centuries associated with black magic ceremonies. The Holocaust can be seen, in a way, as mass ritualistic murder on a huge scale. The Nazi acts were not really so wanton or insane; the Nazis knew quite clearly what they were doing and why: the rituals were required for them to continue to gain and hold power.

The Kabbalah teaches that a consequence of embarking on such a forbidden path is very dire: one's soul can be completely obliterated. In such a case, not only is the person's body destroyed, but his soul as well.

THE EVENTS PRECEDING CREATION

Let us briefly examine the steps leading to creation. We have already looked at the concept of *Ain Sof*, and have seen that *Ain Sof* is as different from the spiritual as it is from the physical. From *Ain Sof*, we are told, a light emanated; in Hebrew, the term is *Ain Sof Ohr*. There was also the "vacated space". That was the next step. The vacated space can be conceptualized as all-black. Imagine a big box, filled with the light of *Ain Sof*. Somewhere, in the light of *Ain Sof* is the vacated space, which is really a very tiny dot. Then, into the vacated space came a line of light.

The dot contained everything that we know about—all the universes, not just the one we know. It contained everything that we can possibly comprehend. It held four universes, of which the physical is the lowest. In this context, highest and lowest do not mean "good" or "bad", but rather distance from *Ain Sof*.

To recapitulate, what existed at that time was *Ain Sof*, the light of *Ain Sof*, the vacated space, and one thread of the light of *Ain Sof* entering it and terminating in the dot. The dot consisted of the "step-down stations"—like a transformer—bringing the energy from each higher universe to the one right below it. When we go out at night and gaze up at all the planets and stars, we must remember that all this is inside only one dot. And all this comprises only a single universe. Three others exist too. This conceptualization begins to provide a way to understand where we stand in terms of our relationship to *Ain Sof*.

Now *Ain Sof* is unchangeable. But the instant that the vacated space came into being *Ain Sof* made the decision to abide by the laws governed within it. Above the vacated space *Ain Sof* is unbounded by logic. Even within the vacated space He is unbounded by logic until the *Sefiroth* are created; logic begins with the *Sefiroth* on down.

For instance, our universe should seemingly have a ten-day cycle of Creation, because there are ten *Sefiroth*. But there is only a seven-day cycle because we can relate to only seven of the *Sefiroth* at all.

There were ten "sayings" in Creation, ten times in which "God said". Why? Because each of the *Sefiroth* was participating in the act of Creation. There were Ten Commandments because each *Sefirah* was involved in the divine system of laws. There were Ten Plagues in Egypt. Kabbalists teach that this was the one time in history when God stated that He would manifest in a certain way so that all humanity could see the manifestation. Ten Plagues: each of the *Sefiroth* had its "turn". Throughout the Bible, we can see the recurring theme of tens. Whenever we come across this reference, we should immediately think of the ten forces of Creation.

Another point this approach clarifies is the anthropomorphic descriptions of the Bible. The text speaks of God and says, "And God came down and looked," or "God's right arm", or "God heard". Such descriptions seem to portray God as if He were a human being. But Kabbalists insist that these are allusions to the *Sefiroth* and that we possess qualities akin to them. The *Sefiroth* created man in their image, so man creates in his image. For example, when the Bible mentions the "right hand of ", it refers to a certain *Sefirah—Chesed*. A description of God's "head" or "leg" refers to another *Sefirah*. Once we possess this understanding, then we gain a much deeper appreciation for what is really occurring in the Biblical narrative.

Another key point must be mentioned now, because we are about to enter into a discussion of paradoxical issues. We have already indicated the Kabbalistic principle that the *Sefiroth* function in an essentially logical way. As reflections of the *Sefiroth*, we humans can operate by logic and thereby presumably understanding all the workings of the *Sefiroth*: stars, planets, gravity and everything else. But what about aspects in the cosmos that do not seem logical? Is everything indeed amenable to logic?

Jewish mystics explain that *Ain Sof* created the *Sefiroth*; they, in turn, function according to logic. However, that which is beyond the *Sefiroth*—or even some of them—is not bounded by logic. *Ain Sof* can do whatever He wants.

Thus, before the realm of the *Sefiroth*—which is the first universe, closest to *Ain Sof*—there existed *Ain Sof*, the light of *Ain Sof*, the vacated space, and the thread of light. At the bottom of the thread of light, the *Sefiroth* came into being.

FREE WILL

We have explored in this chapter several key topics of the Kabbalah. It is now time to confront a fundamental issue: if man truly has free will, then how can God know what will happen? And if God knows what is going to happen, then how can man possess free will? In terms of our analogy, if we see the child is about to put his hand in the fire we will take his hand away at the last second. However, we can not really know whether the child would have placed his hand in the fire.

The fundamental question then becomes: does God know beforehand whether we will remove the child's hand? If the answer is no, then our basic definition of *Ain Sof* is wrong. If the answer is yes, then how much free will do we really have? If everything is already planned, then where does free will enter? How can free will coexist with God's foreknowledge? Keep in mind that this issue does not involve the concept that God must *do* anything about the foreknowledge. Rather, the mystery is this: if I know with one hundred percent accuracy what someone will do tomorrow—and I cannot be wrong—then where does his free choice come in? If God knows before the person was even born that he was going to do something, how much free choice does he possess?

Certainly we cannot compromise with the notion that God is all-knowing; that concept is fundamental to Judaism and the Kabbalah. Simultaneously though we are told that from the very beginning of Creation, free will was given to man. From our perspective, to suppose free will we would have to suppose too that God does not know everything, or that God does not exist in the darkness, or that there really is a place where God does not exist. How could God not exist? When the Kabbalah teaches that God vacated Himself from this space, what does this actually mean? How can there be a place where God does not enter?

Someone might legitimately ask this troublesome question: what difference does it really make in our lives if God knows or does not know? True enough, it may not make a difference to us because we do not possess foreknowledge. It is like going to the racetrack where the races are fixed. We do not know what the fix is, and we can still bet any way we wish. We can still say, "I enjoyed the race because I did not know what the outcome would be." Or, to use another analogy, today we can easily obtain a tape of a sports match and watch it at home on our television. The game has already been played, but because we do not know its outcome, we can watch it as though it is really occurring now. The outcome of the game is already known. Just because we do not know the outcome, this does not change the fact that there is nothing that could possibly happen to alter the course of the game. It is already known, and it is on videotape.

The next question is: are we living out a divine videotape? Are we in ignorance of the future simply because we have not seen the end of the movie? Or, do we really possess free choice so that we can suddenly say, "No, I am not going to ruin my life this way. I am going to change right now," and thereby alter the ending of the movie?

The question seems clear. Either we have free choice and there is no foreknowledge or there is foreknowledge and no free choice. In philosophy, this state of affairs is known as a paradox. It is a situation in which two opposites exist at the same time. Logically, a free will and divine foreknowledge cannot coexist. Logically, the notions that God is everywhere and also that God created a vacated space cannot coexist. Logic tells us that both statements cannot be true simultaneously. This question is the ultimate paradox in all philosophy; every paradox in theology becomes an example of this paradox. No answer has ever been advanced that is logically satisfying. The only answer that seems to make sense to us is that the paradox simply exists on a level above logic. Therefore, logical thought can grasp it only to a certain extent; beyond that point, logic cannot understand it.

There is therefore no way to logically understand this sort of paradox, because it is by nature metalogical. Also, *Ain Sof* is not bounded by logic, since He created logic itself. *Ain Sof* can say: "From this point on, I will play the game according to these rules. But everything that exists out here is beyond the reach of logic." In terms of our diagram, all that lies within the dot of our universe operates according to logic. But that which lies outside the dot is beyond our comprehension. Even the thread of light that comes in is incomprehensible, not to mention the vacated space and *Ain Sof.*

Thus, the only explanation we can give for the paradox of free will and divine foreknowledge is to say that it exists on a metalogical level and is beyond logical comprehension. Through meditation, though, we can travel beyond the confines of the little dot; but we cannot travel through the use of logic. If we wish to commune with the thread of light or with things outside the dot, then it is important for us to meditate and make those leaps beyond logic.

When we examine the vacated space closely, we find that it contains darkness—and many paths through it. Any path that goes through the dot will ultimately come into the light. There are an almost infinite number of paths, in fact, but nearly all are forbidden to us. But there is only one path that comes through the thread of light: that of the Torah. This is why there are so many rituals, regulations, and meditations on the path of Torah and Kabbalah; they are all meant to take us through daily life up into the bigger light of *Ain Sof.* Certainly it is possible to choose another path, but it is very easy to become disoriented in the darkness and to lose our way forever. It is like trying to get out of a desert: one walks in circles and is lost there. Therefore, those who enter the dark space are at great risk of not being able to get out of the darkness.

To make this clear, think of the vastness of the universe—of the millions of light-years that separate us from far distant stars. Then, remember that the entire cosmos is only a little dot; the vastness of the black space is much, much greater. One could spend billions of years literally wandering in this black space and never find the light.

The Kabbalah warns that we can fall into the darkness in a number of ways. There are systems such as black magic that deliberately teach specific techniques for entering the dark realm. Or, we can fall into darkness simply by straying from the Torah path. It should also be emphasized that the Kabbalistic path itself is fraught with danger: returning from the light to the mundane world is no simple matter. As the legend of the Talmud records, four sages went into the PARDES: one went mad, one died, one became an apostate, and only one—Rabbi Akiba—emerged from the experience with knowledge and awareness. These are the real dangers that exist. To go into this situation ungrounded or unprotected—or without a guide—is therefore very foolhardy.

THE FOUR UNIVERSES

There are four worlds or universes within the dot. We exist in the fourth or lowest one. It is comprised of two aspects: the physical world and the spiritual world. Most of our universe is spiritual; only a small part is physical. Now, is the spiritual world above us? The Kabbalistic answer is no: we live in a universe that is both physical and spiritual.

The highest universe—starting from number one—has a variety of names associated with it. Sometimes, it is called the world of emanation, sometimes the world of nearness (alluding to the *Ain Sof*), and sometimes the world of intimacy (again referring to the *Ain Sof*). But remember: even this highest world is removed by many steps from the *Ain Sof*. It is separated by the line, the vacated space, the light of *Ain Sof*—all the way up to *Ain Sof*. It is known as the world of nearness because it is most near to *Ain Sof*. The line itself is really a fifth universe, that of *Adam Kadmon*.

THE TEN SEFIROTH

Let us explore Kabbalistic metaphysics a bit more closely. The world of intimacy, nearness or emanation is known in Hebrew as the world of *Atziluth*. It contains the ten *Sefiroth*; because only the lower *Sefiroth* are bound by logic, some of *Atziluth* is metalogical in nature.

All reality is made up of these ten forces known as the *Sefiroth*; each one has a specific function. Also, each *sefirah* has multiple levels and each is infinite in its potency. None of these forces ever appears separately; there are different combinations and each specific combination expresses a different revelation. In addition, each one of the ten contains all the others; our modern concept of the hologram offers a striking analogy to this ancient Kabbalistic notion. These ten forces are responsible for the universal laws in each of the worlds that come below them.

A very important, related concept is that these forces are connected by a "feedback loop" to man. Man is the only creature that possesses this "feedback loop". Therefore, what man does has great consequences in terms of these supernal forces that control the universe. This is a truly fundamental aspect of the Kabbalah and has many practical ramifications for our everyday lives.

We can define the actual word *Sefiroth* in either of two ways, connoting either "counting" or "telling". But we are probably better off by not defining it. Once we assign it an English definition its meaning becomes restricted; if we think of it as a wholly unfamiliar word, then we can obtain a more relevant picture. We must particularly not confuse the *Sefiroth* with anything physical. We may employ conceptual models or analogies pertaining to the physical world, but the *Sefiroth* are definitely not physical.

The *Sefiroth* are completely self-descriptive. Think of the color "red". No other English words can precisely define it; it can really be defined only in terms of itself. In a similar manner, the *Sefiroth* are self-descriptive. They really even lack names, because names and words do not exist in that other universe. It is only from that universe that things are created which possess names. The *Sefiroth* originate in a level beyond names.

However, the reflections of the *Sefiroth* in the lower universes possess names. Look now at the diagram on page 100. There are four columns. On the left the names of the *Sefiroth* are listed. Immediately to the right is a column with English translations of the Hebrew words for the *Sefiroth*. Bear in mind, of course, that the English words scarcely provide true meanings for these terms. The next column contains the ten Names of God that appear in the Bible and their relationship to the Ten *Sefiroth*. The last column contains the Names of God in Hebrew.

What else does Jewish mysticism say about the *Sefiroth*? We have already mentioned how the cosmos was created and is sustained by this set of forces called *Sefiroth*. These are the fundamental forces of Creation or fundamental channels of the Divine Flow. The relationship of the *Sefiroth* to the light of *Ain Sof* is comparable to the way the body relates to the soul: through the body, we express the soul.

Bear in mind that we can never see a person's soul or mind. All we can see is how that soul or mind expresses itself through the body. Thus, through someone's facial expression and behavior we can read something about his soul or mind. But we can never attain direct access to the soul or mind. Analogously, the *Sefiroth* react and through their behavior we can obtain some knowledge about what lies behind them.

Taken together, the Ten *Sefiroth* constitute everything that is from their universe on down. This is because above them lie other factors. But everything we can contemplate or imagine is encompassed by the interplay of the *Sefiroth*; everything we can observe was created and is sustained by them. Each of the *Sefiroth* has its own unique function, so that ten different functions go into the creative process. However, each *Sefirah* has multiple levels and is therefore a very complex entity.

Each *Sefirah* possesses infinite power, certainly in terms of our comprehension of power. However, it is important to understand that a *Sefirah* never appears separately, acting alone. It is similar to the situation of the human body, when one organ never acts independently of the others. There is a fundamental balance that exists. Even if one organ is over-active or underactive, somehow it is connected to everything else in the body that is occurring. Certainly the organ does not act totally by itself.

Each of the *Sefiroth* can combine in different combinations with other *Sefiroth*. For an analogy, think of the genetic structure of human beings: from a relatively small number of genes, billions of different people are created. The total number of possible combinations of each *Sefirah*—or part of a *Sefirah*—with all the others is almost limitless. So just because there are Ten *Sefiroth* doesn't mean that it is a simple matter to grasp them all. All the diversity in the universe is a permutation from these Ten.

Another way to understand this is that each *Sefirah* contains all the others. This model is quite similar to the contemporary hologram. If one had a holographic picture, one could put it into a holographic projector and see an image. Let us say it is a picture of mountains with a woman standing before them. The interesting things about a holograph is that if one tore half the picture and inserted it back into the projector, one would still see the entire image. One could tear the picture into a quarter or an eighth of its original size, but one would still see the whole image expressed through the projector.

What does this mean? It means that the holograph is constructed in a way different from regular photographs. With a regular photograph, the bottom part of the picture is on the bottom and the top part is on top. But with a hologram, every piece of the picture represents information about the whole thing. Each spot of the picture contains information about the entire image. No matter which spot you take, you will get information about the whole picture.

Where can we see an analogy to this situation? Certainly in the human body and its genetic structure. Every cell of the body contains genes which can be used to construct the whole body. Each cell contains information about the whole body. If we had access to any one cell in someone's body, we would have the information about everything else in his body. Theoretically, at least, we could take one cell and clone the rest of his entire body. Thus, the human body functions like a holograph. And if the human body is merely a reflection of the *Sefiroth*, then these must also function as a holograph. In this way, each *Sefirah* contains the information of all the others. Current quantum physics also provides an analogy for us to consider. Nuclear physicists have found that the atom contains sub-atomic particles which they call quantum particles. Let us refer to them as particles A, B. and C. They are made to decompose in a high-speed atomic accelerator. Physicists have found that within particle A are also B and C; when B breaks down, particles A and C are discovered. When C decomposes, A and B are found along with it. Particles A, B, and C are all different, but no matter how much they are broken down, physicists find that A is B, B is C, and everything is everything. This situation is quite difficult for the rational mind to fathom; it almost seems paradoxical.

The *Sefiroth* are based on a similar principle; every *Sefirah* contains all the information about all the others. Not only do they manifest each other differently, but each combination is manifested differently, just as every combination of genes manifests as another human being with its own personality, facial structure, and body type. There are billions of people on the planet and they are all different. In a like manner, there can be billions and billions of combinations of the Ten *Sefiroth*.

The *Sefiroth* are responsible for all the law and order that we see in the universe. Also, they are connected to human beings via a feedback loop. That is, what we do changes them. What they do changes us and we change them, and so there is a cycle of feedback between human beings and the *Sefiroth*. Remember, when the Bible recounts, "Let us make man in *our* image" (emphasis added), where the plural is used, Kabbalists interpret this to mean that the *Sefiroth* are saying, "Let us make man in our image."

Throughout this discussion we have been obligated to use analogies for the *Sefiroth* are beyond logical description. Interestingly, a comparable situation can be found in the Bible in the first chapter of the Book of Ezekiel. That is, Ezekiel never speaks about seeing things directly; rather, he refers to seeing a reflection of a reflection of a reflection. Later in this book, when we explore a bit of the four worlds, we will observe more closely what Ezekiel is doing in this striking narrative. Kabbalists teach that Ezekiel is starting from this world and working his way up the celestial ladder. He is trying to make a journey inward to the line of light where he could obtain a direct connection to the light of *Ain Sof* and to prophecy itself. Therefore, Ezekiel delineates the steps involved in traversing one world to the next. When we read of how he saw reflections of reflections that is what he is alluding to. Ezekiel does not really call the phenomenon "seeing reflections", but repeatedly comments, "It had the appearance of . . ." This is a very exalted state of spiritual awareness.

CHAPTER FIVE

The Creation Process

THE BREAKING OF THE VESSELS

We have already seen that the Kabbalah teaches that evil preceded good in Creation, that darkness preceded light. But this is only half the story. There is a very intriguing Kabbalistic concept involving the "breaking of the vessels", fundamental to the entire mystical understanding of the Bible. Indeed, this notion is crucial to the whole of Jewish mysticism.

Kabbalists have long taught that when we speak of "what was created first" we must refer to the dot—past *Ain Sof*, the vacated space, and the line. Within the dot there were the ten *Sefiroth*. These can be conceptualized as vehicles or vessels for the flow of spiritual energy through which the other universes would be created. The last universe is our own, which consists of both physical and spiritual aspects.

Kabbalists explain that these ten vessels shattered; they were inadequate to perform the task for which they were designated. They were created to carry a kind of energy which would emanate from *Ain Sof*—through the light of *Ain Sof*—through the light coming into vacated space—and then travel through the Ten *Sefiroth* and create universes. However, when this unimaginably powerful spiritual force passed into the *Sefiroth*, these vessels broke.

The pieces were then brought together and reconstituted. But when this process occurred, they no longer existed as ten

Sefiroth but as five pairs. Thus, the ten became five. These were no longer called *Sefiroth* but *Partzufim*. This is certainly an intriguing account, because here we have almost built into the very design of the universe the concept of something not functioning correctly. How could this happen? Think of the force that emanated from *Ain Sof* as so powerful that nothing could contain it. The function of a vessel or channel is not merely to direct the flow of energy but to contain it. For example, a water pipe directs the water but also holds and limits it. The pipe controls the water's flow and forces it into one place. The *Sefiroth* were not powerful enough to contain—in a sense—God's will. As He willed His force to move, nothing could stand in His way and the *Sefiroth* therefore broke. This analogy enables us to conceptualize why the *Sefiroth* shattered. What is more difficult to conceptualize is how God did not foresee this result in His basic plan of Creation.

Partzuf is actually a Greek word that means "persona". So, now we have five personae. Before we turn to the issue of how God did not foresee this event, there is one more aspect to know so that we do not become confused later on. That is, even though the ten *Sefiroth* broke and became five *Partzufim*, Kabbalists refer to the *Sefiroth* anyway. Why is this? There are really two reasons. One is that we are discussing a spiritual dimension. Not only *Ain Sof* is spiritual, but also what flows from *Ain Sof* downward is spiritual.

In the spiritual dimension, time does not exist as it does for us in this physical dimension. In the spiritual dimension, once something exists, it always exists. An analogy would be an actual filmstrip of someone's life. In the first reel the man is young and vibrant. In the second reel he may be older and weaker. In the third reel he may be dying. And in the last part of the filmstrip he may already be dead. But the filmstrip's reels all exist together at the same time. What matters is simply which part of the film we want to look at. In the same moment of "real time", the filmstrip contains the man's childhood, mature adulthood, and death. All are there at the same time. If we could scan the film instantly, we would see that the events all happen at the same time. But in order for us to understand what is occurring in the film, we must examine it frame by frame. A certain temporal sequence becomes necessary for us to comprehend the film. But the reels all exist simultaneously.

Perhaps a better analogy involves the sequence of logic rather than that of time. Think of a proof in geometry or a statement of formal logic. If "all men are mortal" and "John is a man," then "John is mortal." These are steps in logic, but they do not really exist in time. One statement precedes the other logically but they do not really exist in time.

If, then, the *Sefiroth* existed at one moment in time on the spiritual realm, they will always exist—even though they may be destroyed in another moment of time. Another way to understand this difficult concept is that because *Ain Sof* or God gives existence to all things, then all things are eternal in God's mind. That is, if God thinks about something, then that thing exists in God's mind—just as, if I think about something, it exists in my mind. Everything that God thinks about—all the things that are in the present, the past, and the future—exist in God's mind. Thus, in God's mind, all things exist forever. He has perfect recall of what we call the past; therefore, He must but think of it and it already is.

We are seeking here to find analogies or situations that can help us to understand that which in essence is not logical. This is because part of logic is based on the notion of time. But remember that at the level of the *Sefiroth*, there is no time; time flows downward from them.

Therefore, the Ten *Sefiroth* still exist in their primordial power and also exist as the five *Partzufim* that came from them. They both exist. Admittedly, this is a difficult concept to comprehend; we can think of the matter as simply two different ways in which these forces can align themselves. One way is by acting as ten independent forces. The other way is by combining and somehow functioning as five separate forces.

Let us look at our list. The first one is *Kether*, which will itself become one of the *Partzufim*. *Chokmah* and *Binah* too will themselves each become one of the *Partzufim*. Now, the next six *Sefiroth*—from *Chesed* through *Yesod*—combine to form one of the *Partzufim*. And *Malkuth* will itself become one of the *Sefiroth*.

These five *Partzufim* each have names. One way to name

them is as a family. The first one becomes a grandfather. The second one becomes a father. The third one becomes a mother. The fourth becomes a son. And the fifth becomes a daughter. As separate *Sefiroth*, these forces remain ten individual forces. However, when they recombine or take on another form of the five *partsufim*, they actually assume one persona—a type of personality. It is after these personae that the human personality is modeled.

Now, we must return to the thorny issue of how God did not realize that these ten were inadequate for the task and would break, to be reformed as five. Indeed, this question cannot really stand in this form, because we must say that God certainly knew it would happen. God was perfectly aware of the inadequacy of the Ten *Sefiroth* in their original form to carry out their task. Therefore, this shattering must have been built into God's plan for the universe.

Interestingly, this theme repeats itself over and over in the Bible. We are frequently told that something was created, then destroyed, and that something else came to take its place. We have mentioned the Biblical concept of the firstborn—that often the firstborn is not adequate for the task and must give way to what comes after. Another example is the Ten Commandments. The first set was broken: it was given and destroyed. The second Ten Commandments were then given. This theme keeps recurring in the Bible.

Why did God let the vessels shatter? We have already mentioned the concept of free will. In the basic plan of the universe the breaking of the vessels and their reconstituting allows free will to come into existence. This is because free will depends upon the existence of evil. If God had wanted a system of free will—which was by definition dependent on evil—He could have created an entity such as evil. But apparently this is specifically what God did not wish to do—to create a primary force known as evil. Thus, He started with the Ten *Sefiroth*—all of which were "very good".

When the *Sefiroth* shattered, most of their fragments became reconstituted as five *Partzufim*. But not all of them. Some of the broken pieces fell away from the *Partzufim* and became the essence of evil. Therefore, the Kabbalah teaches that it is from the broken pieces that evil springs. This is now the beginning of the second half of the explanation of evil: that is, from God's perspective there was good first and it was from the breaking of the good that evil came. Evil, then, was created from fallen good. The primary reason for this was so that it could be elevated back again to the good. If evil had existed as an entity unto itself, there may have been no way to make evil other than what it was. But if evil was really broken shards of good, then it would certainly be possible to take them and bring them back to their original source. At that point, they would become good again. This is indeed what Jewish mystics see as the task of humanity as a whole and of every individual. Man's role on earth is to take these broken pieces and, through our actions and way of life, to elevate them back to the source of good. When this cosmic process is completed, all evil as we understand it today will cease to exist. From God's point of view, therefore, first there was good and then there was evil. But on our level, evil came before good; that is why we have darkness preceding light.

FREE WILL

This brings us to a very intriguing issue in the Kabbalah. When we state that God wanted to give man free will, what are we really saying? How free are we and what is the domain of free will? What can we actually do?

Of course, we are not free to do whatever we wish; free will is not a totally inclusive concept. An analogy that may help us here is to conceptualize a person traveling down a river in a canoe. If the river is turning to the right, the man must turn to the right; he cannot turn to the left. If the river is coming to a place that is very calm, the man cannot experience the excitement of the rapids. Or vice-versa. If the man longs for calm while he finds himself in the rapids, he cannot change the course of the river.

In a sense, human life is like that river. Our free will is that, within the confines of the river, we can steer around certain rocks or turn slightly to the right or the left. Or we can pull over to the side and rest sometimes. Or, we can decide when to go on or when to slow down or speed up a bit. Within that river in that canoe we have some freedom and choices to make. But free will is not synonymous with total freedom to do whatever we want.

Rabbi Aryeh Kaplan provided another analogy about the Kabbalistic concept of free will. His analogy is that of a divine chess game. He suggested: imagine that you are playing chess with a grandmaster. The grandmaster can let you make any move you wish and still he will win the game. As a matter of fact, if the grandmaster did not want to end the game in just a handful of moves, he could let you play the game for a very long time. He would certainly manipulate the game in such a way so as to keep you moving and moving. You could not possibly overcome the grandmaster, but he could permit you many, many moves.

Indeed, if the grandmaster decided that your chess bishop should go to a particular square, it would probably not be difficult for him to move his pieces to make your bishop end up on that square. Using this analogy, Rabbi Kaplan compared our daily life to playing a divine chess game. We make a move, God makes a move; we possess total freedom in the moves we make, but God—through the way He makes His moves or countermoves—has tremendous influence on where we will end up despite our seeming freedom to move wherever we want. If we keep this chess game analogy in mind, it can help clarify the concept of free will.

THE SECOND DAY OF CREATION

Let us now look at the Biblical account of the second day of creation. It seems to allude to something about separations of water. The word "sky" in Hebrew is *rakiah*, which is more accurately translated as "barrier". A *rakiah* is a barrier or an interface; either meaning is acceptable. How many times is the word "sky" mentioned? Five times—just as "light" is mentioned five times concerning the first day of creation. Therefore, there exists a parallel between the five skies—or the five barriers—and the five lights. By meditating a bit upon each of the five allusions to "light", and then examining each of the five allusions to "sky" or "barrier", we can uncover several intriguing correspondences that reveal something of the encoded part of the Bible.

Now, what was created on the first day? Light. Day one involved light. Day two is mainly barrier dividing water. Which came first, though? If you look at the text concerning day one, you can see that water preceded light. Therefore, the water being mentioned here is actually the idealized concept of water—the essence of water. This water represents the basic substance from which everything is created. The water is like subatomic particles, but is even more basic to the universe. Kabbalistically, water, as opposed to earth, also represents change. Water takes the shape of whatever holds it. Water cannot be kept as it is unless it is frozen.

Jewish mysticism generally deals with two major aspects: matter and information. In our universe, it is impossible to separate the two because all matter contains information. A book obviously contains information, but so does a chair. The very shape and design of a chair tells us something. Now, can information exist without matter? Can matter exist without information?

It is very hard for us to separate the two, but try to imagine pure matter without any information. That would be the Kabbalistic understanding of this water. It is matter before it has any form, before it is shaped into anything, before we can read any meaning into it, the pure essence of matter. Into this matter information will come; when it does so, then our universe will manifest different things.

Imagine piles and piles of clay. Of course, clay already contains information. But think of the difference between the clay and all the things you could make from it. If you make a pot from it, that pot contains more information than the original clay because it has uses and functions. From the perspective of this analogy, the formless clay would be closer to the essence of pure matter.

The reason that water is mentioned first, therefore, is that it represents the most basic substance. It is easier if we think of this substance not as "water", but as something called *mayim* in Hebrew. The connotation of water for us today is too much related to what emerges from the sink tap.

What do we know of *mayim* from this very first sentence

in Genesis? We are told that God's spirit is connected with *mayim.* From the second sentence, we are given the association of God's spirit with this *mayim.* God's spirit—that certainly contains information—somehow begins to work with this fundamental substance; and from this all things will be created. What was created first with *mayim*? Light. The very first thing created with this basic substance was light. Now, God divides this basic substance; he separates it into two parts, heaven and earth. Or, we can say that he separates it into the spiritual and physical realms. This separation between the spiritual and the physical is quite intriguing, because the Bible next speaks of "taking the waters that are below". Once the separation occurred, then, the shaping of the physical realm took place.

Kabbalists emphasize that since the spiritual and physical originally came from the same substance, there was basic *mayim* and that basic *mayim* was divided. Half of it was made spiritual and half of it was made physical. However, since there was a point in time when the two were the same, there exists the possibility that they can unite, that man can pass beyond the point of separation between the two. This interpretation is just a clue to the meditative knowledge contained within the five mentions of the barrier for the second day of Creation.

From man's viewpoint, the first barrier would be the opposite of light, for "God called the barrier heaven or sky." Then we have the next two as a division: the waters below and the waters above. The first is "God made it" and the second is "Let there be". Remember, the "Let there be" for light relates to a time before it came into existence—coming back to the oneness. These clues can assist us in understanding the five barriers.

Jewish mysticism teaches, then, that behind the duality of all things in the universe lies a unity. Before the duality there existed a oneness and the oneness can still be reached. In this sense, think of the barrier as being nonphysical in nature. A barrier need not be physical like a gate or a fence to be effective. Two people with very different values or ideologies, for instance, may be separated by a much greater barrier than any fence could impose. Beliefs can be tremendous barriers between people. Men and women have died as a result of such barriers.

We can better understand how it is possible to transcend the barrier if we think of it in this way: there was one basic *mayim*, but it became divided into spiritual and physical aspects. In terms of time sequence, first there was the basic *mayim* and then it divided. But if we could travel backward in time we could come to a moment when only *mayim* existed. That is one way to transcend this barrier.

How is such a thing possible? A lot depends on how we conceptualize the world. Let us suppose that the paper we are now reading was a two-dimensional universe. It exists in only two dimensions; it has no depth. An analogy is to cartoon characters which all exist in two dimensions.

Imagine that on the paper universe is one being; diagonally opposite it is another being. These two beings wish to come together. But the time it takes to journey across this universe may be many, many years—just as if we wanted to walk from one continent to another, it would take many years.

But suppose we came to this paper universe from a different dimension. For example, we are three-dimensional beings and could therefore accomplish this feat rather easily. We could take one edge of the paper and fold it over so that it meets the other edge. That folding would take only an instant. Thus, it becomes possible to traverse this great distance in a moment— as soon as we move to a higher dimension. However, a being who is limited to two dimensions would have to move on the two-dimensional plane, and that would take a long time.

Similarly, since we exist in three dimensions, it is theoretically possible for a four-dimensional being—if one existed— to quite easily make things happen that we would find very difficult in our three dimensions. Actually, the fourth dimension is time, so we exist in at least a four-dimensional universe. But if there were yet a fifth dimension, then a five-dimensional being could traverse time in much the same way that we can traverse the space of two dimensions from a three-dimensional existence. The Kabbalah affirms that such a space exists for us.

Another analogy can be offered concerning this somewhat elusive concept. Imagine one circle inside another, drawn on a piece of paper. As long as the circles exist in two dimensions, they can retain their relationship. But the moment we make them three-dimensional—into spheres—the inside one will fall through the outer one. The moment we introduce depth, the inside one will fall through. The circles can be contained only in two dimensions.

Now suppose we had a ball within a ball. How could we remove the inner one without breaking the outer? If we move through time, we could venture back to a moment when the inner ball was not within the outer one. Then we could simply remove the ball from its position and place it somewhere else. Therefore, we can actually take something out of something else by moving to a higher dimension.

Still another way of conceptualizing this matter is to imagine a knot that ties us up in our three-dimensional universe. We cannot make a two-dimensional knot, but if we could move back and forth from the fourth dimension of time, we could escape from the knot. The fifth dimension is sometimes considered that of spirituality or morality—or closeness to God. But we could probably conceptualize an infinite number of dimensions. So all these examples can help us to meditate Kabbalistically on the time when there was only *mayim*—when no separations or barriers yet existed.

The sky is a barrier or *rakiah*. There is also a barrier between the waters, translated into English as "heaven". Now let us return to the first sentence of Genesis. If heaven is a barrier, then what is the barrier there? "In the beginning, God created the heaven and the earth." Thus, the heaven is a barrier between God and everything else. This provides another example of how Kabbalistic insight can help us understand material seen earlier in our study.

The barrier that Genesis describes is not a physical barrier. It can more accurately be understood as comprising beliefs, ideas, or ideologies, which can separate individuals. Another barrier that can relate to Jewish mystical teaching here would be "matter-dependent" and "information-dependent" interactions. Let us briefly examine what this might mean to us.

Let us say that the force of gravity is matter-dependent. Gravity exerts its influence on the density of the material. The amount of information contained by the material does not affect gravity though. A very, very heavy volume—with little information—relates to gravity through its heaviness, not its amount of information. Similarly, a light book that contains much information relates to gravity through its lightness and not through its extent of information. Clearly the information within either book is independent of gravity.

Now, let us conceptualize a kind of force called *ytivarg* ("gravity" spelled backwards) that influences information. It is information-dependent. If something possessed much information, then, that force would act heavily upon it. If something had only meager information, the force would act lightly upon it. But *ytivarg* would be independent of how light or heavy was the object, such as a book.

If two such forces coexisted, there would be an insurmountable barrier between them, for one force relates to matter and the other to information. We can next imagine two separate universes, one information-dependent and the other matter-dependent. They could exist in the same room but never know each other. The two forces could coexist in the same place, each acting completely on its own; each would be totally independent of the other. Each would influence what it influences and would be totally oblivious to the rest. This presents an example of a barrier that does not really separate —the way an ocean is separated from the shore. In this case, both forces coexist within the same space because one barrier is totally unaffected by the other.

Now let us imagine two systems or universes, one spiritual and one physical. Each operates on its own rules. The two realms could coexist in the same place at the same time, yet be completely independent of one another. The beings, one spiritual and one physical, could walk right through each other and never know it. This is because they operate by two entirely different sets of laws. One being operates by gravity and the other by *ytivarg*.

We can certainly conceptualize two forces that could do this. But now imagine that there is a relationship between them—indeed an interdependence. However, despite this interdependence, it would be possible for a spiritual being and a physical being to be in the same room—to actually move right through one another, and not know each other at all. This is because they operate by wholly different laws or principles. Only a being that could perceive both sets of laws would know that both of these were present at the same time. This complex way of thinking is quite central to the Kabbalistic view of the cosmos. Kabbalists have taught for centuries that the spiritual world is right in front of us—in fact, it surrounds our every step. While this paragraph is being read at this very moment, there could be another being in the room also reading a book about mystical ideas. Many different systems could theoretically exist in the room and not interfere with one another because of the barriers that separate them.

The Worlds of Creation

To return to the text of Genesis, we have already highlighted the five lights and the five barriers. Interestingly, there are also five waters that are mentioned in the first chapter of the Bible. Therefore, we can meditate on these five waters as we have done with these other "fives" of Creation.

If *mayim* is the basic "stuff" of Creation, then it must have five levels to correspond to the five universes. Now, remember: first there is *Ain Sof*, then there is the vacated space, and then into the vacated space comes a line of light. Then, a dot is created and within this dot are four of the universes. The line of light itself is the fifth universe, so that the vacated space is surrounded by the light of *Ain Sof*. The first universe is the line that comes into the vacated space. Within the dot are the other four universes.

We have already seen that this line is known as the universe of *Adam Kadmon* in Kabbalistic terminology. This term is rarely discussed in detail in introductory works on the Kabbalah; typically, just the four universes within the dot are described. With reference to these four, then, this universe is that of "emanation" or "nearness" or "intimacy". The second universe within the dot is that of "creation". The third is that of "formation". The fourth is that of "making" or "action". These, of course, are translations from the Hebrew.

Thus far, we have briefly explored two of these universes. That of emanation or intimacy is the realm of the Ten *Sefiroth* or the five *Partzufim*. The universe of action or making is that which we inhabit and it encompasses both the physical world we know and the spiritual world.

What are the two worlds of creation and formation? Think of our existence as predicated upon a certain cosmic "blueprint", and that our mental functions are patterned according to this blueprint. Kabbalists teach that if we can understand our own inner structure, then we can reason from that back to the basic plan of the blueprint.

For example, before we perform an act, we first have to *think* about it. Next, we can talk about it. And finally, we physically behave. Therefore, thought, action, and speech together constitute one way to conceptualize the lower three universes. What would the highest universe be like? It would involve something above or beyond thought.

Where does thought come from? That is a major philosophical question. I have a thought. But where did it originate? Where did this question come from? The question itself is a thought. One answer that philosophy traditionally provides is that will precedes thought. So we can think of the highest universe as a realm of will—also, as a realm of no-things. Thought is already a thing. The realm above thought is that which is beyond things. Or, we can call it a place of nothing, of nothingness, of the Void. From the nothingness comes a thought; from the thought comes speech; from the speech comes action. This is one way to conceptualize the four universes.

Another way to conceptualize them is in terms of computer language. *Adam Kadmon* would be the programmer, the one who writes the program. Above the realm of thought or emanation and nearness would be the axioms fed into the computer. The realm of creation would be the central processing unit, the C.P.U. The realm of formation would be the communication link that exists between the C.P.U. and the final piece of equipment, such as a sensing device or some peripheral component that runs the computer.

Now, we have already discussed the notion that a stepdown system was needed to mediate the unimaginable power of *Ain Sof*. Somehow the incredible energy radiating from *Ain Sof* must be brought down so that we can exist at our ordinarily very low level of cosmic strength. Therefore, we can think of these universes as step-down stations arranged in the following manner: here is the first one and the second one; the line of light is the third; within the dot are the fourth, fifth, and sixth "stations"; finally, the human realm is the seventh "station" and it is also within the dot. By this point, the power of *Ain Sof* has become so attenuated that we can exist as separate points of being.

THE SEFIROTH AND NAMES OF GOD

Sefirah		Name	
Keter	Crown	Ehyeh Asher Ehyeh	אהיה אשר אהיה
Chakhmah	Wisdom	Yah	יה
Binah	Understanding	YHVH (read Elokim)	יהוה (אלהים)
Chesed	Love	El	אל
Gevurah	Strength	Elokim	אלהים
Tiferet	Beauty	YHVH (read Adonoy)	יהוה (אדני)
Netzach	Victory	Adonoy Tzevaot	אדני צבאות
Hod	Splendor	Elokim Tzevaot	אלהים צבאות
Yesot	Splendor	Shaddai (El Chai)	שדי (אל חי)
Malkhut	Kingship	Adonoy	אדני

Above are listed the Sefiroth and the ten Names of God. Look at the third one, which is composed of four letters. In Hebrew, these are the *Yod*, the *Heh*, the *Vov*, and another *Heh*. In English, the Name is often written as Y-H-V-H. It is a very special name of God, one never pronounced in Judaism as it is written. The diagram also indicates that the third and sixth Names of God look similar to one another; they are spelled the same but pronounced differently. Be aware that the true pronunciation of the fifth Name is *Elokim*. The true pronunciation of the third Name is not *Elokim*, but sometimes this Name of God is pronounced *Elokim* so as to not pronounce it as it really is.

The sixth name of God is sometimes pronounced as *A-donoy*. When it is given this pronunciation, it has a different significance than when it is pronounced *Elokim*. But in both instances the Name is not pronounced as written.

Y-H-V-H is known as the Tetragrammaton. If you come across any reference in Kabbalistic literature to the Tetragrammaton, this is the particular Name of God being mentioned. The Latin word derives from the prefix *tetra* meaning "four", for four letters. This four-lettered Name of God has very great significance in the Kabbalah; partly because of its significance or sacredness we are not even allowed to pronounce it.

The Tetragrammaton was pronounced only one time each year, by the High Priest or *Kohen* when he entered the Holy of Holies in the Temple of Jerusalem. This was the most sacred chamber in the Temple and was the site of the Ark and the Ten Commandments. That room was entered only once a year, on Yom Kippur. The High Priest would go in, and as part of the ceremony he would utter that Name aloud. Other than in this one situation—when the holiest individual of the Jews on the holiest day of the year would enter into the holiest place on the planet—never would this Name of God be spoken aloud.

The Tetragrammaton also relates to the four universes contained within the primal dot. The first letter, *Yod*, corresponds to the realm of emanation, nearness, or intimacy. The second letter, *Heh*, corresponds to the realm of creation. The third letter, *Vov*, corresponds to the realm of formation. And the fourth letter, *Heh* again, now corresponds to the realm of action.

Interestingly, the word "universe" in Hebrew has a somewhat different connotation than it does in English. This difference helps to clarify the concept a bit. That is, in English we tend to think of a "universe" as a self-contained unit. But in Hebrew, the word "universe"—*Olam*—means "concealer", "to conceal" or "to hide". For this reason, Kabbalists regard that each *Olam* or universe conceals a higher truth. Thus, from our universe of "making", these other realms are "concealers" —they all conceal higher truths. As we journey through each universe, we draw closer and closer to the highest or ultimate truth. Indeed, the first chapter of Ezekiel, which we have briefly examined earlier in this book, can be seen as a description of how the Prophet Ezekiel traversed these different universes. He narrated how he crossed the various barriers and penetrated what each concealed.

The relevant Hebrew terms for the four universes are the

following: *Aziluth* is first, *Beriyah* is second, *Yetzirah* is third, and *Asiyah* is fourth. These terms are important in understanding what next follows in our look at the first chapter in Genesis. This is because each of these words is used in a specific context. For instance, sometimes the Bible employs the word *beriyah* to signify "create". Sometimes, the Bible says that He "formed" and sometimes it says that He "made". We tend to read these terms almost interchangeably in English: God created, God formed, God made. But Kabbalists see each word as communicating a very precise aspect of Creation.

Let us briefly recapitulate. The Bible relates that light was created on the first day. What is the essence of light? It expands; it fills all the space that contains it. This quality of light thus conveys something of the essence of the corresponding *Sefirah*: that of *Chesed*. It is the fourth *Sefirah*. If the essence of the first day, therefore, has something to do with light which is expansive and filling, then the *Sefirah Chesed* can be conceptualized as unlimited giving.

The next *Sefirah* is *Gevurah*, strength. The strength is somehow related to the concept of holding back and of serving as a barrier. A relevant, ancient Jewish saying is that in order to become a judge and certainly a member of the *Sanhedrin* or High Court of the Jewish nation, one had to be strong, wise, and wealthy. To some people such criteria seemed very unfair. Why should a judge have to be wealthy? Doesn't this criterion discriminate against all those who are not wealthy? And why should a judge be strong?

The answer is that such criteria have traditionally been defined in very specific ways within Judaism. The *Mishnah*, dating back to the early third century C.E., declares that "He who is strong is he who conquers his desires." Thus, one who overcomes his desires is considered strong. The *Mishnah* similarly explains that, "He who is wise is he who can learn from every person." Lastly, "He who is wealthy is he who is satisfied with his lot." So within these time-honored definitions of strong, wise, and wealthy, we see the true qualities necessary for a Jewish judge.

Returning, then, to the *Sefiroth*, we observe that the first day of Creation embodied the attribute of unlimited expansion; the second day embodied that of limitation and of barriers. We will see that the third day involved an integration of these first two.

Clearly, within the process of life, we need both qualities. We need expansion and we need holding back. Without expansion, we would have no growth of new bodily cells and indeed no new life at all. Without holding back, however, we would have unrestrained growth such as cancer. The balance between these two forces is very important.

THE THIRD DAY OF CREATION

There was no "it was good" on the second day; this statement was omitted altogether. However, on the third day, it occurs twice. Why is that? Kabbalists offer many interpretations for this feature in the narrative of Creation. One relates to the notion that if "water" is basic matter without information, then on the second day nothing was really communicated; there was no information conveyed, just formless matter. Therefore, there was no statement that "it was good" until the word "land" is mentioned in the text. "Land" refers to solid matter and with it information could be inserted and "good" could thus exist.

The synthesis of matter and information is life. Where do we find life beginning? On the third day. This day is number six on the list—the *Sefirah* of *Tifereth*. In essence, then, the work of the second day was not completed on the second day—until there was "land" or solid matter. That is why the Bible has no statement "it was good" in reference to the second day.

Now we all know about the famous sin involving Adam and Eve and their eating from the forbidden Tree. But it is not commonly known that this was not the first sin recorded in the Bible. There was a sin before it and it occurred on the third day.

"God said the waters under the heavens shall be gathered to one place, and dry land shall be seen." Notice that He is referring to the waters under the heavens now, the heaven being the barrier between the physical and the spiritual. Thus, the Bible is alluding to what happens on the physical plane. "The waters under the heavens shall be gathered to one place, and dry land shall be seen." It happened. "God named the dry land earth and the gathering of the water he named seas. God said, 'the earth shall send forth vegetation, seedbearing plants and fruit trees that produce their own kinds of fruit with seeds shall be on the earth.'" It happened. "The earth sent forth vegetation, plants bearing their own kinds of seeds and trees producing fruit containing their own kinds of seeds. God saw that it was good. It was evening and it was morning, a third day."

What kind of tree does God mention? The Bible states, "seedbearing plants and fruit trees". Thus, we are hearing about fruit trees. But do we see in the next sentence "fruit trees"? No, we see "trees producing fruit". What is the difference between a fruit tree and a tree which produces fruit? Kabbalists insist that even such a minor distinction in the text must be taken quite seriously. God says that there shall be a fruit tree, but the next sentence relates that the earth brought forth a tree which produced fruit.

Jewish mystics have explained this seeming contradiction in the following way. A fruit tree is a tree which is literally fruit. Certainly such a viewpoint is not how we would think of a fruit tree, but rather as one that produces fruit. But the traditional notion is that people could literally eat the tree; the tree itself was the fruit. Thus, God said, "Let there be fruit trees" meaning the trees would themselves be fruit, but what resulted was something different—trees producing fruit. In other words, a violation of God's plan occurred on the third day of Creation. The spiritual forces that controlled the earth brought forth something divergent from the deity's wishes.

Somehow, life on this day of Creation exercised its own freedom of choice and changed God's plan. Of course, the sin that will pertain to humans will come from a tree and fruit. So the stage had already been set, in some sense. There was already a disobedience to God at this level and it will be compounded later with Adam and Eve.

Bear in mind that even with this violation of God's wishes, He said that "it was good" on this third day. If it was part of God's plan that evil be introduced into the earth to allow free will to exist, then obviously from God's perspective the day was "good". Even after the sin of Adam and Eve on the sixth day—which we will soon examine—God said that "it was good". From God's perspective, remember, there is no true difference between good and evil; it is only from our vantage point that such a difference manifests itself.

A chief highlight of the third day of Creation is that for the first time God's decree is not actualized. And it is interesting that this event occurs: 1) on day three; 2) in relation to a living substance; and, 3) involving a tree and fruit, which will then set the stage for another sin. Somehow, God's plan was for the tree itself to be fruit—the Hebrew expression is *etz pri* ("tree-fruit")—but nature did not cooperate. It is almost as if the tree said to God, "Wait a minute, this is my space. I am going to have a bark to protect myself. I'll give you fruit you can eat, but you're not going to eat me."

How the tree would perpetuate itself is an issue that we cannot even comprehend. This is because had it done what God had asked, then the entire universe would obviously have been different. The later scene with the fruit tree and Adam and Eve would never have taken place. So the whole universe took a turn right there. When life was introduced, somehow it exerted its own will on Creation.

THE FOURTH DAY OF CREATION

We come now to the fourth day of Creation. The *Sefirah* called *Netzach* is associated with it. This Hebrew term is often translated as "victory", "permanence", or "overcoming". What is created on this day? Essentially, the heavenly bodies. Certainly, in terms of our concept of permanence, we can see a connection to the heavenly bodies. They are very predictable. We can predict with tremendous accuracy where the planets will be a thousand years from now. We know precisely where they were a thousand years ago. They function according to well-defined laws. They do not vary in their behavior, unlike fruit trees or people.

Kabbalists teach that up to this day of Creation, the sun and moon were actually taking the primal light mentioned on day one and somehow processing it and sending it to earth.

There was a relationship between the light mentioned on the first day and what is said about the light that emanated from the sun and moon. If we look at verse sixteen, we can see that it says, "Two great lights". These refer to the sun and moon. Now, it is interesting that the disk size of the sun and moon—as they appear from earth—are exactly the same size. Astronomically, this is quite improbable. Since the earth, sun, and moon are all such different sizes, the spacing among them would have to be very precise for this to occur. Some astronomers have suggested, in fact, that the probability for this to have happened by random chance is infinitesmally small—that some other force must have been involved.

The Midrash relates a very intriguing account of this day. The story is about the sun and moon. The Midrash recounts that originally the sun and moon were the same size. However, the moon came to God and said, "Listen, you can't have two rulers of the same size ruling the earth." So God said, "All right, if that's the way you feel about it, make yourself smaller." And the moon was forced to become much, much smaller than the sun.

Kabbalists see two separate ways to understand this account. The first is relatively simple: that God punished the moon for complaining about its equality to the sun. Further, Kabbalists say that this story relates to the primary feminine and masculine forces in the universe. From this perspective, the sun represents the male principle and the moon the female principle. Initially, these basic forces—the male and the female—were supposed to be coequals. But the female principle sought to dominate and take over the male. As punishment, God said, "All right, then, we will make you smaller, and you will become subservient to the male principle." This is one way to understand the story of the sun and moon.

The other way to regard it is that the moon was right about the ineffectiveness of having two equal rulers in power; that it is not possible to have this arrangement for long. From this view, the moon was correct in asserting that the female principle must dominate for the universe to exist. Think of the Kabbalistic cosmology about the "vacated space". The only way the universe could exist was for the "vacated space" first to be formed—to block out some of the infinite light energy of *Ain Sof.* This process implies that the entire cosmos depended on the dominance of the feminine principle. Therefore, when the moon came and pointed this out to God, He said, "You're right, and you must now make yourself smaller." In this regard, the shrinking was not a punishment but quite the opposite. Think of the moon as somehow refining and fine-tuning the sun's light and sending it downward to earth. From this view, the moon became something like a fine-tuning device—a very important function.

We can also meditate on this story for our personal development. In order to become closer to God, we must take our individual ego and make it smaller. We have to diminish our ego to draw closer to the divine. This account teaches the lesson that shrinking something is not necessarily a punishment, but that it may allow that aspect to come to a greater truth beyond.

Thus, God was saying to the female principle, "You are right, and you must dominate the male principle in this universe. But the way you will dominate is to make yourself smaller, because in so doing you will draw closer to the truth." Also implied in this narrative is that the moon possessed a greater wisdom and cosmic sensitivity than the sun. We are given an intimation of this notion by the fact that it was Eve, the woman, who reached first for the Tree of Knowledge. This issue we will examine soon.

THE FIFTH DAY OF CREATION

The fifth day is number eight on our list—*Hod* or "splendor". Another definition of *Hod* is "submission" or "giving in". *Hod* refers to a kind of dependency, but one that maintains its integrity. This situation would be the opposite of a dependency in which one loses his or her integrity to the dependency.

What happens on the fifth day? Fish and fowl are mentioned on day five. Keep this in mind when we think about what *Hod* represents. Also, verses twenty and twenty-one mention for the first time the word "soul"—"living soul" in Hebrew. Verse twenty states, "And Elokim said: 'Let the waters

be filled with creatures that have a living soul (or soul living)." "
Parenthetically, the Kabbalah teaches that there are three
types of soul: the animal soul, the vegetable soul, and the
spiritual soul. All animals possess an animal soul. All plant
forms possess a vegetable soul. Human beings, though, possess all three. The spiritual soul is comprised of five parts—
each part of Him contributes another aspect to this soul.

On the fifth day of Creation, Kabbalists traditionally hold
that God destroyed one of the two sea monsters said to exist
on the planet at that time. To prevent them from reproducing
and spreading, God killed a living creature. This was the first
time in the sequence of Creation that death was manifested.
This is not mentioned directly in the Biblical text, but is nevertheless part of the ancient oral tradition associated with the
Kabbalah: that death was introduced on the fifth day.

The *Sefiroth Netzach* and *Hod*—relating to days four and
five—are traditionally connected to prophecy in the Kabbalistic system. This immediately suggests that it may prove
beneficial to meditate on the events of days four and five,
especially if we wish to better understand prophecy. The allusions are to heavenly bodies, fish and birds, and prophecy. We
can also use verses four and five as a *mantra*, to help gain the
power of prophecy: just repeat the verse over and over, pref-
erably in Hebrew.

THE SIXTH DAY OF CREATION

The sixth day of Creation is associated with the *Sefirah*
called *Yesod* ("foundation"). On this day man was created. Man
is seen as the foundation of the universe. Kabbalists teach that
the whole essence of Creation—all of these steps and all of
these universes—were designed for the sake of human existence. All the other realms of the cosmos were created simply
to filter downward the divine power so that humans can deal
with it. In this sense, too, man is a microcosm of the universe.

The famous verse twenty-six is contained here: "Let us
make man in our image." We have already mentioned one interpretation of this cryptic remark—that it refers to the image

of the *Sefiroth*, because they were speaking. However, the letter *Beth* here can mean "with" as well as "in", as previously discussed in reference to the first word of Genesis. Remember that twelve interpretations can be gleaned just from the first word of the Bible. We have seen that "With the beginning" can apply just as the phrase "In the beginning". Therefore, the passage in verse twenty-six can mean, "Let us make man with our image," imparting a very different understanding.

In the first chapter, only the name *Elokim* is mentioned. As we have seen, *Elokim* represents the five *Partzufim*; it comprises five letters, each relating to a *Partzuf*. Now verse twenty-seven states, "God thus created man with His image. In the image of God, He created him, male and female."

Thus, the Bible states quite clearly that His image is male and female. This is actually the first definition of the divine image, and notice that it comprises both male and female. Kabbalistically, this indicates that of the ten *Sefiroth*, half are associated with the male principle and half with the female principle. Unfortunately, in English we tend to speak of God in the masculine sense. But the Bible very tersely suggests that the deity represents for us an androgynous gender.

Through the Tree of Life structure, we can conceptualize the right *Sefiroth* as masculine and the left as feminine. The center *Sefiroth* are androgynous. For instance, the *Sefirah* of *Tifereth* mediates between *Chesed* and *Gevurah* and is a combination of the two. Similarly, *Yesod* is the combination of *Chokhmah* and *Binah*. Therefore, when we think of God we should clearly conceptualize the deity as both male and female.

Another interesting feature concerning the sixth day of Creation involves verses twenty-nine and thirty. They convey a statement about vegetarianism—that human beings did not eat animal flesh in the Garden of Eden. Kabbalists teach that after the Flood in Noah's time this situation changed. Men and women were permitted to eat meat, though slaughtering was to be done humanely. We will turn to this subject later, as it involves a deeper understanding of the chain of events that led from Adam's creation to Noah. Indeed, the whole issue of who Adam was (for Jewish mystics teach that he was *not* the first human) is a very important one.

The Seeds of Evil in Creation

It may be interesting for us to briefly note that something "went wrong" on each day of Creation. What was "negative" on day one? The formation of darkness. On day two? The barriers. Also, there is no mention of "good" regarding this day. Thus, there is an absence of good and the divine work was not completed. On day three? The fruit tree episode occurred then. On day four? The conflict between the sun and moon, and the reduction of the moon's power. On day five? The formation of death. On day six? The narrative about Adam and Eve.

By reading the Bible very closely in this way, we can begin to see the origins of evil and of the negative in the universe. Clearly these aspects of darkness permeate the whole fabric of Creation; they occur not simply on one day but on all of them. On every day of Creation something negative is produced.

God's Naming and Creation

There is another interesting feature of the biblical account of Creation that can serve as the basis for a meditation as well. This is based on the observation that God names only four things during Creation. Because there were seven days of Creation, we might initially think that God names everything, especially since the text begins, "God said, 'Let there be light,' and there was light." We are likewise told that "God called the light day." The same description is provided for the second day. God names only four things: dry land (earth), heaven, the sea, and the day (light).

Now why are these four specifically named by God? Other aspects of Creation are certainly mentioned, but they are not specifically named by God. In meditation, remember not to think of light as something that emanates from a light bulb in a room. Try instead to feel something of the essence of light, the essence of day, and this will surely bring you to a closer understanding of the divine message for us.

THE SEVENTH DAY OF CREATION

The seventh day, of course, is the Sabbath day. Within Judaism and the Kabbalah the Sabbath is a day of tremendous significance. Many rules and regulations surround and infuse it. Therefore, when we come to speak about some of the practical applications of Jewish mysticism, we will look closely at the Sabbath day and see why we must act quite differently on it.

For now, let us turn to chapter two, verse three. It states, "God blessed the seventh day and He declared it to be holy. For it was on this day that God ceased from all the work that He had been creating, so that it would continue to function." Here we have another example of the difficulty in accurately translating the Hebrew into English. This popular English translation is not quite accurate, for in Hebrew the word "created" is in the past tense, but the next word, *la-asoth*, means "will make in the future". Thus, the Hebrew really says, "which God created to make in the future". The *la-asoth* is clearly something not yet completed; it is something to be made.

Thus, instead of translating this passage as "all the work which God created and made", we should read it as "all the work which God created and that needs to be made". This allusion to that which needs to be made in the future refers to our human role in the cosmos: completing the process of creation. If we look at the diagram, we can see that this world—*Asiyah* is the fourth world, the world of man, and it is precisely this word that is used to describe it. It is for us to finish the work which God began in Creation.

Now, it is important to note that Chapter One of the Bible concludes with the sixth day and that Chapter Two begins with the seventh day. We should recall that these chapter demarcations were made by the Greek translators. The Hebrew Bible was not written in chapters. If we examine a Torah scroll —which is the way the Bible was written—there indeed seem to be paragraphs, but not chapters. We will find entire sections and then an indentation, and then another paragraph begins. Kabbalistically, these paragraphs are understood as the sections that God dictated to Moses. A hiatus was marked by the indentation denoting a new paragraph and relates to a place where God and Moses paused. These places of pause are very important for Kabbalists, but they are not chapters. It was the Greek culture that divided the Bible into chapters, so that the first chapter ends with the sixth day and the second chapter begins with the seventh day. The Greeks regarded the seventh day as encompassing rest and inaction, therefore necessitating a new chapter.

The Kabbalistic approach is to continue Chapter One through the first three sentences of the Greek Chapter Two, and then to begin Chapter Two with the fourth verse. It states, "These are the chronicles of heaven and earth when they were created on the day God completed earth and heaven." Interestingly, this verse employs a different name of God and this is very significant. Also, the second part of this fourth sentence transposes the order of heaven and earth. A contradiction seems to exist.

The first part of the sentence says, "first heaven, then earth". The second part says, "first earth, then heaven". So which really preceded the other? This single sentence has historically generated considerable controversy in Jewish mysticism. Around it has revolved the key question: Is the spiritual dependent on the physical? Or, is the physical dependent on the spiritual? The resolution of this issue produces for Kabbalists a very different relationship between physical and spiritual than that which our culture typically embraces.

Also, this sentence employs the word "made", as opposed to "created". The Hebrew actually says, "On the day that God made earth and heaven". Instead of the word "created" as the Bible indicates in Chapter One, here the word "made" is used. Why is this so important? Because it concerns the particular level of Creation being discussed; "created" refers to one level and "made" to another.

The next chapter will closely examine the whole account of man's creation on the sixth day. We will see that there are two separate versions of what occurred. How Kabbalists traditionally reconcile these two is quite interesting. In part, they teach that the Bible narrates two different accounts because it is referring to two totally different aspects of Creation. When we understand these differences, it will be immeasurably helpful. For instance, it will serve to clarify the seeming confusion about the age of the universe already mentioned earlier in this book. It will also serve to clarify why Adam was *not* the first man and how we are to understand such statements as that made by Cain after killing his brother Abel, "If I go out they will kill me." Who would kill him? And, what was one of Cain's first acts when he left the Garden of Eden? He built a city. Who was he building it for? His behavior clearly implies that there were many people. Where did they come from all of a sudden?

As we will see, Kabbalists provide us with a very different picture of this biblical narrative. One clue for all this is the Hebrew word *eleh* in the fourth verse of Chapter Two: "*These are the chronicles . . .*" Whenever the word *eleh* appears in the Bible, it always indicates the start of a totally different narrative. Here the word is employed to announce that something new has started.

THE SEFIROTH AND THE DAYS OF CREATION

Let us now return to the account of Creation and place it in the context of the *Sefiroth*. Each day of Creation is under the primary influence of a particular *Sefiroth*; however, the highest three *Sefiroth* are beyond this universe and are not involved in its divine process of Creation. Number four—which is *Chesed*—is the *Sefira* most influential in the first day of Creation. *Gevurah* is the most influential for the second day. *Tifereth* corresponds to the third day; *Netzach* the fourth. *Hod*, *Yesod*, and *Malkuth* correspond to the fifth, sixth, and seventh respective days of Creation.

Perhaps a helpful way to understand the *Sefiroth* and what they are about is to look more carefully at the first chapter of Genesis and see what was created on each of these days. We can try either as a meditation or as an intellectual exercise to ponder the essence of that which was created on each day. As we do this, we begin to obtain a perception of what each *Sefira*

is and what it influences in our universe. Such an approach is
certainly more useful than simply looking at an English translation of the terms and saying that *"Chesed* is love."
We must remember that the Bible does not contain any
real mention of God, only of the *Sefiroth.* These are the Names
of God that appear throughout the Bible. When we see a particular Name used, we must associate it with its corresponding
Sefira; this approach will help us to better understand the true
meaning of the Bible. For example, when God reveals Himself
to a patriarch or prophet, we note what Name He uses. His
Name to Abraham is different from His Name to Moses. Kabbalists interpret this to mean that different attributes of the
Sefiroth are communicating with these holy figures.

THE PURPOSE OF CREATION

To summarize some of the concepts of this chapter, a
primary starting place for all Kabbalistic teaching about
Creation is belief in God, *Ain Sof.* Indeed, using the Ten Commandments as a model, the statement: "I am God" demon-
strates this underpinning. Another basic Kabbalistic notion
is that there is a purpose to Creation; it was not a haphazard
or chaotic event. Related to this idea is the acceptance that
there are some aspects of Creation that are accessible to the
human mind—and other aspects that are not.
Therefore, since we cannot "psychoanalyze" God or attempt to figure out what was in His Mind, we are left only with
the manifest features of Creation. Jewish mystics say that
what is clear is that one purpose of Creation was for the *Ain
Sof* to bestow good on humanity through a series of step-down
channels. God wanted to bestow good on human beings for,
in the Kabbalistic understanding, humanity is the center and
purpose of Creation.
Now the highest form of good—almost the only pure form
of good—is *Ain Sof* Himself. Therefore, to bestow good really
means to attach oneself or to allow another person to attach
himself or herself to *Ain Sof.* In essence, that is the Kabbalistic
notion of the purpose of Creation: for each of us to draw nearer
to God as best we can.

CHAPTER SIX

Eden and the Human Condition

THE RIVERS OF EDEN

Chapter 2, verse 8 of Genesis describes how God put the man that He had formed into the Garden of Eden. But if we follow the text closely, we see something very unusual between the tenth and the fourteenth verses: all of a sudden we start to get a description of the Garden of Eden. We are told that there are four rivers and that they have certain directions of flow. When this description is completed, then the biblical narrative resumes. If we follow the biblical account carefully it seems that this description of the four rivers is totally out of context. They are never mentioned again, nor do they relate to anything that has come before. The description suddenly appears in the middle of everything.

What does the Kabbalah say about the four rivers? The number four is, of course, significant. There are four letters of the Tetragrammaton, four universes, four basic elements of Creation. The four rivers, then, have a symbolic significance: they indicate that there is a never-ending flow from the Garden of Eden out into our world. Before the Bible finishes the story of the Garden of Eden, it tells us that there are four rivers that come from the Garden, go out into the world, and connect to us. In other words, our connection to the Garden of Eden remains through these rivers and waters.

The Bible affirms that despite the separation between

humanity and the Garden of Eden, we have a connection to that level of formation. In physical terms, the *mikveh* (ritual bath) expresses this connection. A book entitled *The Waters of Eden* by Rabbi Aryeh Kaplan, is strongly recommended. It discusses in detail this concept of the four celestial rivers and the *mikveh*—and what all this has to do with our daily lives.

ADAM, EVE AND THE TREE OF LIFE

Right after the account of Adam's creation comes the story of the Tree of Life and the Tree of Knowledge. Let us focus on this narrative, because Kabbalists have seen it as very important. Remember, the Garden of Eden contains a Tree of Life and a Tree of Knowledge. God tells Adam not to eat from the Tree of Knowledge, but that he can eat of all the other trees in the Garden.

Kabbalistically, the Tree of Life is a time-honored name for an arrangement of the Ten *Sefiroth*. Thus, the Tree of Life is viewed as a spiritual ladder: in the middle of the Garden of Eden was this spiritual ladder comprised of the Ten *Sefiroth*. They were arranged in such a manner as to form a ladder that one could use for spiritual growth.

That ladder had three pillars to it. The middle one was called the Tree of Knowledge. This was the one that Adam was told not to eat from. Of course, in Hebrew the word is not "knowledge". Rather, it is the word *daath*, which means "to join". Once we understand that, the whole account becomes far more clear. So this was a Tree of joining or connecting.

We can now forget the typical interpretation that eating of the Tree of Knowledge would give Adam the awareness of the difference between good and evil. Kabbalists teach that Adam already knew this, that the Tree had nothing to do with this distinction. Rather, the Tree had to do with *joining or connecting to good and evil*.

Evil already existed at that time. There were several reasons for its existence, the primary one being humanity's need for free will. But until that point in time, evil existed *outside* of man. It was not part of his nature. Man was not attached to good and evil. There was good, there was evil, and there was man.

To partake of this Tree would be to connect to the good and the evil. Thus, the question was really one of becoming attached to good and evil, not of knowledge of good and evil. It would seem that at God's level, God could be attached to good and evil and not suffer from that. But when man becomes attached to good and evil, and develops this bond as an internal reference, then all kinds of problems result.

Before that time, other people were attached to good and evil. But Adam and Eve were to be founders of a new species. Thus, we can add two other features to Adam: he had the ability to speak directly to God, and he lacked an attachment to good and evil. Of course, it is no accident that the Hebrew word *daath* also means to connect or join sexually: therefore, to "know" biblically is also to relate sexually.

Human Mortality

The Kabbalah teaches other intriguing notions about Adam's prohibition from eating of the Tree of Knowledge. In verse 17, God says, "On the day you eat from it, you will definitely die." But did Adam die on that day? No, he did not. What, then, does God's remark mean? Kabbalists have offered several explanations. One is that "on the day" refers to a God-day, since it is God who is talking. A God-day is a thousand years. How long did Adam live? Nine hundred and thirty years. There is a whole story about seventy years of Adam's lifespan being given to King David. Thus, God was declaring that Adam would live one thousand years if he ate of the Tree.

Another explanation is that "On that day. . .you will definitely die" means that the *death process* would begin. Not that death would finalize on that day, but that the death process—the built-in aging of our cells—would begin to move toward death. Bear in mind, God's initial plan was for Adam and Eve to have been immortal. This is a fundamental concept in the Kabbalistic view of the account of Adam, Eve, and the Garden of Eden.

Now, in verse 18, the first "not-good" of Creation is mentioned. Prior to this, God has said ten times that "it was good".

Of course, the fact that this is God's eleventh saying is significant. What is this first "not-good"? That it was not good for man to be alone. And what is the remedy for this condition? The creation of woman.

If you look at the biblical passage carefully, you will see that it is logical. In verse 17, God says the equivalent of, "Don't eat from the Tree or you'll die." In the next verse, He says, "It is not good for man to be alone." Why is it all of a sudden "not good for man to be alone"? Because if there is no death, if man is immortal, then it is not so important that he have a partner with whom to propagate the species. If Adam were a single immortal being formed differently from all other humans, and if he had a special mission to fulfill, there would be no need for another person. But the moment that the possibility of death enters, then he needs someone else. For he may fail in his mission—which, in fact, he does.

An additional teaching is that the return of the human body to dust is not the end of the story: the Kabbalah is emphatic that the human body will be resurrected. In fact, resurrection relates intimately to the coming of the Messiah. This is why many messianic tales describe an individual's death and resurrection, the most famous being that of Jesus. In the Messianic Age resurrection will play an important role as will the former physical body.

Kabbalists emphasize that we have both a spiritual and a physical part to our inner nature. The soul represents the spiritual part, though it encompasses several levels. It is the divine part of the soul that binds man to the highest spiritual root.

Once Adam sinned, then God issued the dictum that "on the day that you eat from that Tree, you will die". This is because Adam had now incorporated evil into his being; it no longer lay outside of himself. At that point it became necessary for man to die.

Yet the Kabbalah clearly expresses the notion of the body's resurrection. It has for centuries taught that the soul and body constitute one unit. The higher, divine soul is somewhat limited by the body, because these portions of the Self must restrict their attachment to the physical world. Dreams are one gateway to the divine soul, but generally we do not have access to these exalted levels.

Kabbalists suggest, though, that the body returns to dust and remains part of the dust of the earth until some future time. At that time, the dust will be re-formed into a body again and reunited with the soul. Then the body will be in the same state as was Adam's body prior to his sin. Each human body will be free of the evil within it. This transformation will herald a whole new world and a whole new life, beyond anything we can imagine. The Prophets say that these events will happen after the coming of the Messiah.

From this perspective, we can see why cremation is forbidden within traditional Judaism. The idea is that the body should return to the dust from which it came. Ashes are somewhat different from dust.

In Chapter 3, verse 22, the Bible next mentions the Tree of Life. What did the snake say would happen if Adam ate from the tree? Here is the verification that the snake was right. What does God say after that? That man must be prevented from putting forth his hand and also taking from the Tree of Life.

Bear in mind that the Tree of Life was not forbidden to Adam because he was to be immortal anyway. But now that immortality was to be taken away from him, there was a danger that he might run to eat from the Tree of Life. Therefore Adam had to be removed from the Garden of Eden.

This biblical comment teaches us that the Tree of Life had something to do with immortality or prolonging life. Knowing that the Tree of Life can be seen as a meditative focal point, we can conclude that the *Sefirot* can serve as a meditative focus to extend one's life. For remember, the Tree of Life was not really a physical tree but a spiritual force. Today we have access to both the Tree of Life and the Tree of Knowledge; through meditation we can utilize these spiritual forces.

Reincarnation

Though the Kabbalah stresses the reality of resurrection at the coming of the Messiah, it also embraces the notion of reincarnation. In fact, the topic of reincarnation is very much a part of historical Judaism. For centuries Kabbalists have clearly taught this intriguing doctrine.

The classic Jewish teaching is that each soul has a particular, unique mission to accomplish on earth. Until it completes this mission, the soul must continue to incarnate on earth from lifetime to lifetime. Of course, this view is quite similar to the the well-known Far Eastern notion of reincarnation.

However, there is another Kabbalistic concept about reincarnation. This concept is associated with Rabbi Isaac Luria ("the ARI"), one of the most important mystics in Jewish history. Rabbi Luria's notion is a little different from that of other Kabbalists, but it has had many adherents.

Rabbi Luria taught, in essence, that a person does not keep receiving different bodies in which to reincarnate. Rather, the individual receives only one body and has one lifetime to experience it. After that lifetime, the soul can reincarnate again; however, the entire soul does not always reincarnate. This is because it may be the *neshamah* that has to do certain things; or, it may be the *ruach* or *chayah* that has to do certain things. It is possible for the entire soul to reincarnate; but it is also possible for different sections of the same soul to reincarnate simultaneously in different people.

What does this complex notion mean in terms of reincarnation? Rabbi Luria's concept is that the soul will choose a body that already has its own soul. The soul that is doing the reincarnating is seemingly "going along for the ride" in this other body. In other words, think of a particular soul with its body—it has certain tasks to perform and certain life experiences to undergo. The other soul may be assigned to that body to "piggyback" onto that individual and vicariously learn from that individual's experiences.

Thus, according to Rabbi Luria, a person has his own soul. At the same time, there can be other souls attached to that person; these other souls are there to learn certain things. Usually these souls do not interfere with the person's inner life, but at times they can do so. On rare occasions the things that occur to a person happen because the "hitchhiker" needs a certain experience—not because of the person's need. Also, the "hitchhiker" usually stays for the whole "trip". Bear in mind, too, that the "hitchhiker" is not a new soul. We don't receive new souls in this celestial process. When we first hear this idea, it appears strange. We almost have to sit with it for a while before this concept begins to acquire personal significance. Who arranges this whole process? That issue relates to the entire cosmic system, and it is beyond our discussion for the moment. However, there are many, many Kabbalistic books on this subject. Rabbi Luria himself said that he was writing a whole volume based on *gilgulim* ("cycles"); his disciple Rabbi Chaim Vital set forth these principles in a fascinating work called *Sefer Gilgulim* (*Book of Cycles*).

The question is sometimes raised whether there are any references to reincarnation in the written Bible. There are indeed references, but no direct statements. That is, the oral Bible tells us that Moses had three separate incarnations. There was the one of Moses, and two prior existences: first as Abel or Hevel (Cain's brother who was killed) and then as Seth, Adam's next son.

If one reads the Bible closely, one will see in Chapter 2, verse 7, "And Adam knew his wife again and she bore him a son and called him Seth, for God has appointed me another seed instead of Abel. . ." This is the only biblical reference to one person substituting for another. Adam had many children, but this was one singled out specifically to substitute for Abel. Thus these two children were two incarnations and Moses was the third.

Chapter 2, verse 7 also talks about "a living soul". This is because the "living soul" is a reference to a soul on the level of *chayah*—living. The verse also says the soul is living. How does the soul become living? By being attached to the body. This is the other important lesson we learn from this single verse—that the soul gains existence by becoming attached to the physical body. Once more we see the dependency of the soul on something physical in order to have a life of its own.

The topic of reincarnation in Jewish mysticism is vast. To summarize, the Jewish view is rather different from the traditional Far Eastern one. Two points need to be emphasized: 1) reincarnation is very much a part of Judaism and fundamental to the Kabbalah; 2) there are at least two distinct Kabbalistic doctrines on the concept: the first is akin to the Far Eastern view that the same soul has a succession of bodies; the other, advanced by Rabbi Luria and his adherents, is that the body is a vehicle for the soul in which to have certain experiences—there is a primary soul attached to the body, but there can be other souls there too as "backseat passengers".

THE ANIMAL KINGDOM OF EDEN

Let us look next at Chapter 2, verse 19, for it teaches us two interesting concepts. Adam has already been created, and animals are described as coming after him in existence. This statement seems to be the direct reverse of Chapter 1. In the earlier chapter, the Bible recounts the evolutionary process by which animals were created and then evolved into humans. But in Chapter 2, in this special place—the Garden of Eden—a man is formed and then animals are formed. Therefore, Kabbalists say, the Bible is really describing the level of formation.

These animals are in the realm of formation, as opposed to the physical world. Consequently they will be different from the animals that we know. What characteristics do we know from the Bible itself about these animals? First, they are all vegetarians. And second, they are not aggressive. They do not eat one another, nor do they fight with one another. This situation is a foreshadowing of the prophecy of Isaiah, "The day will come when the lion will lie down with the lamb. . ." Isaiah is telling us what will happen in the Messianic Age, that there will be a reverting back to what God's original plan had been. We see, then, that in the original plan the animals were different from today's animals, just as Adam was different from later humans.

A significant feature of Chapter 2, verse 19 is that we have man naming the animals. The naming of things is very important from the Kabbalistic perspective. Remember, the naming of a spiritual force brings it down to the physical plane. Thus Adam is very involved in the creative process of these animals. God initiates the process, but then lets Adam name the animals.

What is involved in the naming? As was mentioned earlier, the name is seen to contain all the animal's qualities, like its entire genetic pattern. In order for Adam to name them, he had to understand the very essence of every animal species that existed. He had to understand the very root of each one so that he could bestow the appropriate name.

THE VEGETABLE SOUL

As was explained earlier, according to the Kabbalah there are three types of soul: animal, vegetable and spiritual. Humans possess all three. It is perhaps unusual to think of a vegetable soul, but plants are living, and everything living has a soul. Therefore, there is a certain soul-level which is characteristic of plant life. Higher forms of existence, such as man, also share those levels. Each of us has the ability to relate well to the entire plant kingdom on a soul-to-soul level.

Perhaps we can see a good example of this capacity in certain cultures where people use herbs for healing and spiritual development. In such cultures, men and women not only employ herbs medicinally, but sit and meditate with the plants, almost communicate with them. We even hear today of people who talk to plants and have a rapport with them. Kabbalistically, we can say they are in touch with the vegetable level of their soul and communicate on that level with plants.

THE MARRIAGE OF ADAM AND EVE

We return now to Adam in the Garden of Eden and his need for a partner. Chapter 3, verse 21 sets forth the famous biblical account of how God took the rib of Adam and turned it into Eve. However, Jewish mystics have long seen matters rather differently. First, they do not translate the word as "rib" which immediately changes the whole narrative. The Hebrew word means "from his side". So we have the word "side" and not "rib". Kabbalistically, Adam was a hermaphrodite. Adam and Eve were originally one being. They were attached almost like Siamese twins, back to back. This situation created very poor communication between them, so the two sides were separated. One became Adam, the other became Eve. Now, in Chapter 3, verses 23 and 24 relate, "And the man said, 'This is now bone of my bones and flesh of my flesh. She shall be called woman because she was taken out of me." That is what they are called. The Hebrew word for man that is used here is *ish* and the Hebrew word for woman is *isha*. If we look at the Hebrew, we will notice that these two words share two letters and differ in two letters. They differ in *Yod* and *Hay*. Interestingly, if we combine these two letters we have formed a name of God. Without the name of God, the Hebrew word means "fire". Kabbalists interpret this to mean that male-female relations are by nature very fiery, unless we can get God back into the relationship. Each partner brings a part of God to the relationship so that together they form a complete name of God. Without the divine presence, there is only fire.

To complete this notion, verse 24 relates, "A man shall therefore leave his father and mother and be united with his wife, and they shall become one flesh." Thus, here we have the concept of man and woman uniting and becoming one flesh. The notion is that Adam and Eve were literally one flesh but were separated and came together in marriage. This is why marriage is a holy union, for God has been brought back into the male-female relationship.

THE NACHASH ("ENCHANTER")

Now we come to the very strange narrative in Genesis about the snake that does all sorts of things in the Garden of Eden. But do we know it is a snake? We must go back to our basic principle, which is to look at the Hebrew terms. The Hebrew word is *nachash*. Let us say that there is a *nachash* in the Garden of Eden that does these things. We do not know what a *nachash* is, but if we don't think of it as a snake, then our understanding of this account will be more clear. If you think of a snake, then your associations make the whole narrative into only a bizarre tale.

In Hebrew, *nachash* can mean "enchanter", "magician", or "witch doctor", not only "snake". Those are all valid translations for the word *nachash*. If we use any of these other translations, we already have a different feeling and sense of the biblical or Kabbalistic account. Regardless of the English translation we prefer, we must keep in mind that the *nachash* is a very high spiritual force. It is functioning on the level of *Yetzirah* ("Formation") and is a very high spiritual entity.

In Chapter 3, verses 1 and 2, the Bible says, "The serpent was the most cunning of creatures that God made. The serpent asked the woman, 'Did God really say that you may not eat from any of the trees in the Garden?' The woman replied to the serpent, 'We may eat . . .'"

Now, what does the *nachash* say to her? And what does she reply? Did God say, "You may not eat from any of the trees"? She answers, "We may eat from the fruit of the trees of the Garden, but of the fruit of the tree that is in the middle of the Garden." God said, "Do not eat it, do not even touch it, or else you will die."

So we have here an interesting addition. Did God tell Adam not to touch the tree? There has been no mention until now of not touching it. God said to Adam, "Don't eat of that tree." Somehow, though, Eve obtained the message, "Don't eat it and don't touch it." Kabbalists have interpreted this apparent discrepancy to mean that Adam, in his concern that Eve might eat from the tree, decided to make the prohibition even stricter. Therefore, he told Eve, "Don't touch it." In a sense, he felt that he would improve on God's work by making the rule even stricter than God had made it.

Kabbalists say that the *nachash* soon after pushes Eve against the tree and nothing happens to her; thereupon she becomes more willing to eat of the tree. Adam, then, had inadvertently set her up by giving her the extra-strict admonition. This point is very important in understanding the divine punishments that later follow. From the Jewish mystical perspective, this aspect of the narrative is also relevant to the human condition, for it teaches that there is a danger in making rules stricter than they need to be.

For example, one could logically say, "I don't want them to eat this, so I'll say, 'Don't touch it.'" Then someone else could come along and say, "Well, you don't want to touch it, so don't even go into that room.'" Still another person could say, "Don't even go in the house," and before we know it, we have a whole series of rules upon rules upon rules. Eventually people will start to question and then break these rules that are three and four times removed, and nothing happens. So they begin to discard the whole system, with disastrous results to follow. If they had simply observed the initial rules, as given, these difficulties would not have taken place.

To return to the Biblical account: despite the fact that the *nachash* pushed Eve against the Tree and nothing happened, somehow the *nachash* had to convince Eve to eat from the Tree. What kind of argument could it muster to accomplish this? Remember, both Eve and the *nachash* were spiritually lofty beings. In Kabbalistic terms, she was hardly the naive woman that popular myth has portrayed.

In fact, Adam and Eve were very, very special. They were created by God separate from all other humans; they were not simply the product of evolution. They possessed the gift of prophecy. They spoke directly to God. Their level of prophecy was higher than any people who would come after them; even Moses required a trance state to speak to God. Adam did not; it was part of his nature. Likewise with Eve. If we think of their spirituality in modern IQ terms—and genius is an IQ of perhaps 180—then their IQs were over 500. Their degree of spirituality was beyond anything we can conceive. Thus, it is not such a simple matter for the *nachash* to approach Eve and sell her a bill of goods.

According to the Kabbalah, the *nachash* persuaded Eve by essentially saying,

> The most important thing in your existence is to get closer to God. You're here to elevate humanity, to help it draw nearer to God. That is your function.
> Now, how can you do that? There is really only one way, and that is by emulating God. The more you are like God, the closer you will be to God. Therefore, if you really want to fulfill your destiny and get close to God, you must become like God.
> What characteristics does God have? God is unbounded by any laws or rules. Why, then, do you suppose God gave you this rule? Do you think God cares whether you eat from the Tree or not? Obviously not. The only possible reason God could have for putting forth this prohibition is to give you

the ability to break it, and become completely free. The only way you can be completely free is to disobey God.

Let us consider the *nachash*'s argument for a moment. The Bible relates that he said to her, "You will be like God if you eat from the Tree." In other words, that she will become God-like by emulating God. Eve goes ahead and eats from the Tree; after all, the argument is very logical. The *nachash* was right. There are two paths for drawing closer to God: one indeed is by emulating Him; the other is by obeying Him. The real question is which way is more important, to emulate God or to obey God?

Think in terms of a parent and child. The same situation exists. A child can learn by emulating the parent, or by obeying the parent. There may be certain things that the parent feels the child is not yet ready to do; the child must not emulate the parent yet. Thus, the parent will give rules and the rules will be different from what the parent does. The parent may say, "You must go to bed at eight o'clock." But the parent stays up until eleven o'clock. Part of the message that the parent must communicate in child-rearing is, "Do as I say, not as I do." However, the child constantly watches the parent and wants to be like the parent as much as possible.

So there are two ways of becoming like an adult. One way is to imitate adults and learn from what they do. The other way is to obey adults. Now as parents we understand that most of what we teach children is through our own actions—how we speak to our husband or wife, how we treat others, how we view the world. This is probably the most profound teaching children learn from their parents. Therefore, emulating is a very significant way of becoming an adult.

Nevertheless, there are also times in maturing when we must simply obey parents. God's argument relates to this issue. God does not claim that the *nachash* lied or fooled Eve, because it did not lie. God counters that the issue was one of obedience. He says, "From the Tree that I told you not to eat, from that Tree you ate." This point is really emphasized repeatedly in the Biblical account. Part of free will is taking responsibility for your actions.

Now, what is Adam's response to God when God says to

him, "Did you eat from the tree that I told you not to eat from?" What does Adam reply? He says, "She did it." He blames Eve. Jewish mystics see this as a very ungrateful response, because Adam shows no gratitude to God for the woman. In fact, he blames God *and* the woman. For this response—some Kabbalists say *only* for this response—Adam is punished.

Why is the *nachash* punished? As we have seen, the devil is really only a faithful servant of God. We can recall here the story of the king's son and the woman the king hires to seduce his son. Now, what would happen if the woman confided to the young man that she had merely been hired to tempt him? Suppose she said to him, "Look, the king just hired me to do this. I'm really not bad." This comment would negate the whole purpose of the son's test.

The *nachash* conducts himself in this same way. Instead of testing whether Eve will obey God, he tries to use her desire to obey Him as the means to make her partake of the tree. God wanted the issue to be one of loyalty and the *nachash* confused this issue. The *nachash* undermined the task God had given him. Just as the king would punish the hired woman for undermining his instructions, so too does God punish the *nachash*.

This is a very important point. Nowhere in the Bible is the *nachash*'s argument refuted, because it essentially told the truth. But the *nachash* overstepped its bounds by telling Eve that she could express her loyalty to God by partaking of the fruit. It should have simply challenged Eve to disobey God, as the means to test her obedience to Him.

The entire Kabbalistic notion about the capacity for angels to engage in evil really pivots around this point. Unlike man, an angel is not connected to anything evil. It has no evil urge. But sometimes an angel, in its desire to draw closer to God, will seek to do more than it is supposed to. It is not that the angel is deliberately seeking evil, but that it does something more than God asks. In this act, the angel falls.

Kabbalists say that angels possess some modicum of free will, but are completely devoid of the evil urge. Therefore, angelic free will is seen as very limited compared to human free will. In short, this narrative teaches us the notion that we can inadvertently be "too good". Adam tried to be too good by telling Eve not to touch the Tree of Knowledge. Then the *nachash* tried to be too good by doing his job too well.

But what specifically was Adam's sin? Did he know that he was eating from the forbidden Tree? The Bible simply states, "She took some of its fruit and ate it. She also gave some to her husband and he ate it." It is clear that Eve knew what she was doing because she believed the *nachash*'s argument. But what about Adam?

There are several ways that Kabbalists look at this issue. One notion is that he ate of the Tree that God had told him not to eat of. Another concept is that Adam did *not* know that he was eating from that Tree. However, he certainly showed the sin of ingratitude, for he responded to God by saying, "The woman that You gave me did it." Indeed, some Kabbalists have suggested that this comment was Adam's only sin—that he did not commit the sin of eating and that ingratitude was his misdoing. Others have insisted that both were Adam's sins. The issue ultimately depends on whether you think that Adam knew what Eve was giving him to eat.

FIGHTING GOD AS A PATH TO SPIRITUAL POWER

In the same vein, the later narrative in Genesis of the Tower of Babel illustrates the concept of how people can fight God as a deliberate means to gain spiritual power. In brief, the Bible says that the people of old wanted to build a tower to ascend to heaven and fight God. That is a very strange idea. How could humans build a tower to heaven and combat God? Of course, we could dismiss this account by simply concluding that these were very primitive people who really believed that they could build a tower up to heaven and strike at God.

But this notion is not so primitive. Actually, there is something very sophisticated about it. What could it possibly mean? Before we can answer this question, consider the later Biblical account concerning the nation of Amalek. Right after God had delivered the Jews from Egypt, amidst "all the signs and wonders", Amalek suddenly attacked them. Egypt, the strongest military power in the world, could not overcome the Jews. Yet this little nation, Amalek, came out to battle with them.

Jewish mystics tell us that all these accounts are linked. What, then, is the motivation behind Amalek's attack, the building of the Tower of Babel, and the *nachash*'s argument? Simply, the motive behind the whole path of black magic: to reach God through the pursuit of evil. This is known as the path of emulating God as opposed to obeying Him. God is all-powerful and beyond our understanding of good and evil. Therefore, the motive behind the path of darkness is to become Godlike by seeking total power and going beyond ordinary good and evil.

The idea of fighting God is that you engage in a battle that you knowingly cannot win. But the point is not to win; it is to become closer to God by combatting Him. In the very process of fighting God, you are exerting and exercising your Godlike qualities to a very high degree. By complete, total defiance of God, you are emulating His limitless power.

Thus, the builders of the Tower of Babel did not expect to defeat God. Nor did the nation of Amalek expect to defeat the Jews. In both cases, these people were resigned to losing their struggle. But in their very process of combatting God, they understood that they would be drawing closer to Him.

These are the two pathways for becoming closer to God. One is the path of the *nachash*, the builders of the Tower of Babel, and the nation of Amalek. This is known as the way of total emulation of God. The other path lies in obedience to God. That is why God says to Adam that the real issue is one of obedience. God does not deny that Adam can reach Him through emulation; nor does he dismiss the *nachash*'s argument as foolish or untrue. But God says, "I told you not to take that path."

God gave humankind certain laws and said, "Follow these." Thus, one way of attaching to God is to follow the rules that He put forth for us to follow. The second path is that of emulating God. Although the path of obeying God is the primary means, it is important to be able to do both—to obey God and to emulate God.

Jewish mystics further teach that for this good to be bestowed on humanity, we must earn it. The good is not just handed to us. To earn it requires the existence of free will. In order to present us with the means to do good, God gave humankind the Torah as the "owner's manual" or spiritual handbook to earthly life. Kabbalists consider this text as giving us step-by-step directions to the path of holiness. Such directions are meant to help us become constantly aware of God and to bring us closer to Him.

ADAM AND EVE'S SEXUALITY

A basic Kabbalistic interpretation is that an immediate consequence of eating from the Tree of Knowledge was an increase in human sexual drive. The Bible tells us that before this event occurred, Adam and Eve were naked and they were not ashamed; sex was a relatively neutral thing for them. But after their sin, sexual awareness increased tremendously and sexual desire surged through them. According to Jewish mystics, Cain and Abel were already born when the eating of the forbidden fruit took place. Thus sex and procreation already existed.

Before this sin sex was really to propagate the species and had little of the desire and fire—the *aish*—that surrounds our own sexuality. At that time humanity was immortal, and immortal beings have no need of a strong sexual drive. However, when man eats of the tree his mortality begins. Sexual desire must be strong now to insure the survival of the species. Thus, the first consequence of eating of the tree is an increased sexual desire.

But what fruit was it? What kind of tree was it? The Bible does not say. Certainly, though, there is no reference anywhere to an apple. Some Kabbalists have suggested that the fruit may have been a fig, or grapes, or an *esrog*, but none have named an apple. So the apple has been maligned along with the woman.

There is an interesting aside comment here. The Bible says that Adam "hears the voice of God walking". This means that essentially Adam is on a very high spiritual level, and what he hears or perceives is that God is leaving him, walking away. Adam can discern that God is walking away. His connection is going to be very different from this moment onwards. He has gone down a level, and he is going to go down more.

Circumcision

If we look at Chapter 3, verse 21, we may be surprised to learn that it reflects a Kabbalistic teaching. This verse comes after Adam and Eve recognized their nakedness, took leaves and put them on. The Bible says that God made leather garments for them. Once more we have the old problem of what the Hebrew really indicates. The leather is *or* ("skin"). Thus, skin can be understood as leather. What, then, are the garments of skin that God fashioned for Adam and Eve? Jewish mystics explain that it is the male foreskin and the female hymen. These are the skins that God made for them.

The whole issue of circumcision involves a returning of humanity to the pre-sin state of existence. In the process of evolution, human beings had developed a foreskin and a hymen for the two sexes. Apparently Adam and Eve were originally created without these tissues; God fashioned them only after they sinned.

We can therefore add this fourth difference to Adam, as compared to other humans. He lived a long life, he spoke directly to God, he was without a sexual drive, and he had no foreskin. After he sinned, he was given a foreskin, and circumcision was necessary as a rectification for his spiritual decline.

When we discuss the mystical significance of circumcision, a legitimate question immediately arises: why isn't the girl's hymen cut at the same time that the boy's foreskin is removed? In brief, Kabbalists teach that the woman does not require circumcision. She is considered to exist on a higher and more complete spiritual level than a man. The man requires an extra "boost", so to speak, to begin earthly existence at the same spiritual level as the woman.

Modern electrical technology offers an analogy when we refer to a male plug and a female plug. The electrical current as it runs through the house is where the female plugs are. For a male plug to possess any electricity, it must be plugged into the female. But the female is already wired; electricity is running there all the time.

We can think of the difference between male and female spirituality in this way: the female is prewired, already connected spiritually; through circumcision, the male becomes spiritually "charged". For this reason, although women have never been prohibited from performing many of the *mitzvoth* typically assigned to men, they have not been asked to perform these because the sages have regarded them as already existing on a high spiritual level. Women do not need to carry out *mitzvoth* like wearing *tefillin* or a *tallis*. The man must perform the *mitzvoth* to reach that spiritual level; he has further to go than the woman.

Indeed, it is a clear principle throughout the Torah that whenever there was a woman prophet and a male prophet alive at the same time, the woman prophet was always on a higher level than her male counterpart. The Bible states this principle quite explicitly.

THROUGH THE UNIVERSES: THE TREE OF LIFE

Kabbalists teach that everything in the physical world has a counterpart in the spiritual world, and that all are linked. The classic analogy is that of a tree. Interestingly, Kabbalists use trees a lot as analogies, as focal points.

Think of an upside-down tree. Its roots lie in heaven and its branches are on earth. Thus, the spiritual roots exist in the spiritual plane and the branches are what we see in the physical plane. But all the branches are connected through the tree to the root, so that everything in the physical plane has a counterpart in the spiritual world. They are linked together.

Everything in the physical world originates from its roots in the spiritual world, except for one thing. There is one thing that does not originate in the higher levels: man's free will. By definition, our free will is not dictated from above. Therefore, human free will is the one exception to this universal plan.

It is through this characteristic that we each have the ability to change the entire universe. Everything is already predetermined in the spiritual dimension and flows downward into the physical dimension. Animals and to an extent even angels are predetermined. However, since man has free will, he can act independently of the universe's laws. Our free will is not unlimited, but within certain limits we can move in one way or another. What we do, then, will feed back through the tree to the roots; a new cause and effect cycle is thereby created. Of course, there is a paradox here, for *Ain Sof* is surely aware of the changes that we will be making.

THE CURSES ARE LIFTING: PRE-MESSIANIC TIMES

Jewish mystics teach that we can recognize the coming of Messianic times by the lifting of God's curses to Adam and Eve. That is, when the curses begin to lift, that is the beginning of pre-Messianic times. Intriguingly, the curses against both Adam and Eve are now starting to lift.

What was Eve's curse? Essentially, that childbirth be painful and that women be subservient to their husbands. It is certainly possible to have childbirth without pain nowadays. Within our lifetime, childbirth has become much less the seemingly inevitably painful process it had long been. As for the subservient role of women, dramatic changes are obviously occurring in current times. Thus we can clearly see that Eve's curses are lifting within our lifetime.

What are Adam's curses? Basically, that he must earn his bread by the sweat of his brow, that he will have to till the soil. Certainly this situation has been true for humanity until very recently. But now it is no longer true that most of us need to go out and work the ground. When people do so, they now use complicated machinery. Clearly it is no longer by the sweat of our brow that most of us earn our bread. In fact, some of us are earning our bread without much physical effort at all. Adam's curses, too, are lifting within our lifetime.

In short, this condition suggests to Kabbalists that we have entered pre-Messianic times. What does this mean? According to Jewish mystical tradition, it means that it now becomes possible to promulgate the secret teachings and make them public. Tradition teaches that a necessary part of the pre-Messianic period is to publicize the hidden wisdom, as a groundwork for the Messianic Age. Not only, therefore, is it permitted to teach the Kabbalah openly, it is necessary.

This is one of the reasons why more Kabbalists are willing

to discuss this very material. They feel that, to an extent, the whole Messianic Age is dependent on a large number of people knowing these things. This is because such knowledge—and the actions that flow from it—is very much involved in the "feedback loop" of the Messianic Age.

Kabbalists have been concerned, until very recently, about keeping this knowledge secret. They felt that if such knowledge fell into the hands of the wrong people, they would possess this power and use it in a negative way. However, the Kabbalists also believed that in the process of time, there would be a degeneration of morality and of caring about life. They believed, therefore, that when humanity sank to that level of lowness, it would also become possible to teach the Kabbalah openly. This is because at that point, people who were immoral would not take such matters seriously anyway. If a sage came to them and said, "Here are mystical teachings from the Bible!" they would even spit on the material. It would mean nothing to them. But before our present age, many people would have been eager to obtain and use such knowledge.

We are at a time now when one could literally go on television and teach all these esoteric subjects, and many people would simply turn the channel or laugh. The chances that the average person would take this material seriously are remote. But some people do take such knowledge seriously. Therefore, we can see a confirmation of the ancient prophecy that a time would come when one could teach these matters openly, because "the wicked would not listen anyway and the righteous would be listening".

Of course, today there are many spiritual systems available to us. Kabbalists see this explosion of world-wide traditions and methods as quite necessary in the pre-Messianic era. Such pathways help point people toward a higher consciousness. They also induce many to think for the first time about all these matters. Whether through Zen, or Taoism, or Buddhism, people are experiencing a loftier awareness. Such traditions certainly prepare men and women for the insights of the Kabbalah. Without such systems, much in Jewish mysticism would fall on deaf ears.

THE CHERUBIM

At the end of Chapter 2, verse 24, the Bible mentions the story of the Cherubim. Right after Adam and Eve are expelled from the Garden Eden we are told that, "He drove out the man and He placed to the east of the Garden of Eden cherubim and a flaming sword which turned every which way to keep to the way to the Tree of Life."

The Cherubim are mentioned in a few other places in the Bible, mainly in sections that describe the ark in which the Ten Commandments are kept. Around the ark of the Ten Commandments were two Cherubim. It was from between these two Cherubim that God said to Moses, "I will speak to you from between these two Cherubim." This is where prophecy would emanate.

Kabbalists, therefore, observe that the two Cherubim guard the entrance to the ark and the Ten Commandments— and also stand guard in the Garden of Eden. Thus the initiate must get past these Cherubim to enter a higher level of existence. The first chapter of Ezekiel also mentions the two Cherubim. This provides us with a signpost for Ezekiel's level of consciousness—that he had just reached the threshold of prophecy—before he proceeds to recount his vision.

We can thus think of the Cherubim in two separate ways. First, that they are obstacles to overcome. This notion is clear enough. Second, that they represent milestones in our meditative development. That is, when we perceive the two Cherubim in our meditation, we stand at the threshold of a high spiritual level. Their flaming swords, in this light, are like beacons signaling our level of meditation; they do not necessarily have to be interpreted as harmful forces.

This last, brief topic concludes our review of the story of Creation. We have begun to sense the vastness of the Kabbalistic perspective and how many mysteries it encompasses. Now that we have gained this information, what utility does it have for us? It is to this provocative subject that we next turn.

CHAPTER SEVEN

The Way of the Mystic

Let us look more closely at the Kabbalistic view of human existence—especially involving causality and free will—in the universe. If one puts one's hand into the fire, one will certainly get burned. The results are immediate and unmistakable. Cause and effect are clearly linked. Why is it then, for so much of our daily lives, that the cause-and-effect nature of actions is not so clear-cut? Why do we not receive a clear, divine reward each time we perform a good? Conversely, why are we not clearly punished each time we act wrongly? There surely does not appear to be a very direct relationship between our day-to-day conduct and its consequences.

But think about this situation for a moment. If there were such an obvious correlation, then free will would cease to exist. If we were immediately and obviously rewarded whenever we did a good deed, why would anyone ever do otherwise? If we were immediately and vigorously punished as soon as we acted unethically, who would ever risk such behavior? The nature of free will requires that the "payoff" not be so direct as when we place our hand into the fire; the correlation must in a way be more difficult for us to conceptualize.

On the spiritual level, then, the "hand-in-the-fire" situation simply does not hold. We often see that good people suffer tremendously for their convictions, and that evil people reap the enjoyments of life. Jewish mystics teach therefore that God imbued suffering with the power to dispel our insensitivity and bring us close to Him. Suffering is also a way to allow us to become more pure and lucid about the nature of existence. Through suffering, we are forced to change and grow. Suffering has the power to lead us beyond the frontier of pain.

THE KABBALISTIC CONCEPT OF HELL

It is at this juncture that we should explore the ancient Kabbalistic concept of hell. One of the clearest ways of presenting this intriguing notion was put forth by the Baal Shem Tov, founder of Hasidism in the mid-eighteenth century. The Baal Shem Tov was a great spiritual master and teacher. Relying mainly on folktales and parables to transmit abstruse Kabbalistic ideas, he brought the light of Jewish mysticism to the impoverished and uneducated Jewish masses of Eastern Europe. In order to describe hell the Baal Shem Tov related the following story.

Once there was a kingdom in which a king ruled over a vast territory. Many people lived in the kingdom. While they did not have the opportunity to see him or come into direct contact with him, they had much contact with his laws and decrees. Many of these rulings seemed unjust and harsh, especially for the poorer folk who lived in the far reaches of the kingdom.

After a new decree had been issued, one man in particular was incensed over yet another harsh edict. To show his resentment and bitterness against the king, he took a bucket of excrement and smeared its contents on a statue of the king which stood in his town square. He defiled the statue.

At this very moment, some of the king's soldiers happened by and saw the man's act. The next day, the man's deed and name were reported to the king. He instructed his soldiers to bring the man to the palace.

When the soldiers came to the man's house and arrested him, he knew that he had been found out. He imagined that he would now be tortured or decapitated for his offense against the king's honor. He was swiftly brought to the palace and kept waiting, under guard, for quite some time. Finally the king said to his soldiers, 'Take this man and put him to work. Give him a job. Let him work in the gardens of the palace.'

Thereupon, the man was taken and told that he was to

work in palatial gardens. He did not understand this at all, for he had anticipated something completely different. The man was given a place to live, and daily worked in the gardens.

Several months passed. The man reflected that he had a nice house now, nourishing food, and enjoyable work. He found the gardening pleasant and invigorating. In fact, he had never had life so good.

A long time went by. The king said to his guards, 'Remember the man whom we put to work in the gardens? I want you to give him a promotion. Make him the head gardener.' The guards came to the man and announced his new position. He was now in charge of all the people who worked in the garden. He had respect and authority.

A long time went by once more, another year or two. The king said to his guards, 'I want to give this man another promotion. I want you now to move him inside the palace. I want him to have a job here within the palace, a job with even more honor than he enjoyed in the gardens.' The man was approached again and informed of his new promotion. He moved into the palace. He acquired more authority, more money, more power.

Every period of time the man received another promotion. Finally the man was promoted into the king's inner circle of advisors. He found himself at a huge table in the king's inner palace. He met with the king; his opinion was sought by the king's other counselors. He became one of the most powerful figures in the entire vast kingdom.

Of course, during all this time that had elapsed the man had begun to rethink his original deed. Now that he had a chance to be so close to the king, he could perceive him in a very different way than he had been able to before. The man realized how good the king was, how just his decrees were. Now the man was himself part of the king's decision-making process; he understood the other side of the issues.

The story doesn't end here, though. The man kept receiving more and more promotions. Finally he was promoted to be one of the top two or three most powerful advisors of the king. He had become one of the most important figures in the kingdom. He was making decisions that affected the entire kingdom.

One day he happened to be alone with the king. The king suddenly said to him, 'I imagine you are very surprised since you came to the palace.' The man answered, 'Yes, I am.' The king replied, 'This isn't what you expected, is it?' And the man answered, 'No.'

'Well, have you enjoyed your stay here?' the king asked.

And the man responded, 'No, I've been miserable every moment that I've been here. The more good you've done for me, the more miserable I've felt. I have to confess to you what I did a few years ago.'

The man then told the king of his earlier deed against the king's statue, the event that brought him to the palace. He related that now he had come to feel very differently about the king's acts and decrees.

This is the Kabbalistic concept of hell. It is not a place where we are made to suffer, in the sense that other religions portray hell. Rather, Kabbalists view it as a place where we are brought closer to the king, closer to God. In coming closer to God and seeing more clearly what His plan is all about, there will be suffering from within. Suffering will not come from without us but from inside us. It will come from the awareness of what we have done against the king. Yet the suffering borne from this awareness will bring us closer to God. So even hell can serve to draw us nearer to God.

PATHWAYS TO GOD

Now, if we are to really understand the Jewish concept of hell versus drawing near to God, there is one very important aspect to know: that Judaism accepts the idea that anybody can get close to God. One emphatically does not need to be a Jew to be close to the Holy One; Judaism accepts no exclusiveness. It has for millennia taught that any individual, Jew or non-Jew, can achieve the highest spiritual state. Indeed, the Bible is replete with references to sages and prophets who were not Jews. Clearly, then, Kabbalists believe that the loftiest degree of divine communion is open to us all.

As a matter of fact, Judaism has long delineated different pathways to draw nearer to God. Certainly, one path is the Jewish path, but there are a variety of those that are non-Jewish in nature. Kabbalists indicate that these non-Jewish paths are quite viable and effective. If anything, they are easier than the Jewish path, which Kabbalists regard as much more difficult.

However, Kabbalists believe that the Jewish path is incumbent upon all Jews. They do not have the God-intended choice to pursue another spiritual path. Jews must follow the Torah path to achieve true closeness to God, but non-Jews are not required to do so. The reason for this notion dates all the way back in time to the era of Noah and what are known as the Seven Laws of Noah ("Noahide Laws").

There were seven commandments that preceded the Ten Commandments given to the Jewish people. Jews traditionally have considered these to be incumbent on all of humanity. As long as humanity observed these seven commandments, they would be fulfilling all the requirements they need to be close to God.

The Jewish path, however, constitutes many more laws than these seven. We know of at least 613 laws that are incumbent upon Jews, though many of these pertain to the Holy Temple and therefore do not apply to Jews today. In any event, seven is obviously a far smaller number than 613.

Of the seven Noahide Laws some are familiar, others less so. They are as follows: 1) Do not murder. 2) Do not steal. 3) Do not practice idolatry. 4) Do not engage in sexual crimes (a law primarily aimed at incest). 5) Do not take God's Name in vain. 6) Do not eat the flesh of a living animal. (This is the literal English translation, but it has historically been understood more broadly: Do not show cruelty to animals.)

Finally, there is one "thou shalt". It is the seventh Noahide Law and commands that people establish a system of justice where they live, including judges and a formal administration of law. Thus non-Jews have seven general laws to follow; any non-Jew who fulfills these seven in his or her daily life can achieve a closeness to God.

The Kabbalistic Path

In contrast to the Noahide Laws stands the Kabbalistic path. It is very complex with many more laws and many more rituals. Within its general framework are two conduits to spirituality: obeying God and emulating God. The obeying of God essentially means the observing of the laws and dictates of the spiritual handbook known as the Torah. The Kabbalistic path also embraces the practice of meditation.

What is the Torah path? In order to understand it fully, we must return to the question of what distinguishes the spiritual and the physical realms. We have come to the idea that space is of primary importance. If the Kabbalistic goal is to get close to something spiritual, then how can we accomplish this on earth, a physical place? After all, in the spiritual realm there is no space. Remember that when we spoke of a spiritual dynamic, we concluded that two spiritual aspects that are separate cannot come together. So here is a real dilemma: without space, it is impossible to bring two opposite things together.

For Jewish mystics, the way out of the dilemma involves the realization that something spiritual can be bound to something physical. A prime example is the human soul, which is bound to the body. We say that human beings have a soul and that the soul is bound to the body. Thus the answer is that we can take two opposite spiritual aspects and bind them to the same physical object. In this context, good and evil coexist within man, though in the spiritual realm they can never come together because they are opposites. If we take something physical, though, we can attach or bind the urge for good and the urge for evil to the same physical object. Through the physical there is a medium for the joining of these two spiritual aspects.

The same principle holds true for God and man. God and man are worlds apart; the soul is very far from the Holy One. How can these two entities, so far distant, ever come together? How can they ever meet? Kabbalists teach that the only way they can be linked is through something physical, through the human body or some other physical object that both entities can join. For on a purely spiritual plane, it is not possible for these two things to meet. All the meditation in the world cannot bridge the gap. Therefore, only in the physical realm can man and God be brought together. This is a very, very important concept.

From this perspective, the Torah is filled with allusions to specific objects that relate to religious practice. The reason these objects have significance is that God has bound Himself to this object or this ritual. Thus, if man comes and binds himself to the same object or ritual, then through it he will be linking himself to God's binding and ultimately to God. A divine connection will be made. On this theme it is also interesting to note another difference between humans and angels. We are told that angels cannot even imagine a universe above the one they dwell in. They can function within their universe and see everything below them, such as human affairs. But they lack even the concept that something can exist above them. This is because the notion of something that lies above requires that what is above is somehow linked to what is below.

Only the human brain can accomplish this task. Because the human brain is a physical object, it can understand aspects above it—because those aspects can bind to the human brain. Therefore, in this capacity, man has the ability to reach beyond even what an angel can imagine. Once again, this involves the notion of a body that provides a linkage to very high spiritual levels. A spiritual entity, even an angel, cannot progress without a body. The physical body allows us the capability of linking to the very highest reaches of the divine.

Interestingly, it is in this context that the Kabbalah understands the nature of astrology. Just as the Kabbalistic system deals extensively with reincarnation, it also deals extensively with astrology. The teaching, in a nutshell, is this: to exert any influence on the physical realm, even angels and celestial beings must bind themselves to certain physical objects. Otherwise, they would have no way to affect anything physical. Therefore, the heavenly bodies represent linkage points or bindings between the spiritual realm and ours. The stars and planets do not actually influence human individuals; rather, the angelic forces that are bound to the heavenly bodies influence us. In a sense, all the influence flows from the existence of the heavenly bodies like the planets in our solar system. Ultimately, though, it is the spiritual forces linked to them that affect us.

The Mitzvoth

Let us now return to the Kabbalistic concept of the ritual objects in Judaism. We have already mentioned *tefillin*. When a Jew participates in the particular act of using *tefillin*, he is binding himself to a physical object through which there is a linkage to God. The will of God is the same as God. Therefore, if God attaches His will to a certain action and says, "I will my will to be attached to a specific act," then we can effect a linkage to the divine through performing those acts.

Kabbalists approach the structure of *mitzvoth* from this perspective. *Mitzvah* is often mistranslated as "commandment". But the root of the word comes from the word "to bind", because each *mitzvah* is a way of binding ourselves to God. Each represents a special way to bind us to Him, through performing certain acts and using certain physical objects.

Now, remember we have already discussed the numbers 365 and 248. We have seen that the arrangement of the Ten *Sefiroth* as personae consists of 365 channels and 248 limbs or parts of the body. The total comes to 613 and this number is also the sum total of all the *mitzvoth* set forth in the Bible. Each *mitzvah* thus relates to an integral part of the *partzuf*. Since the *partzuf* is what creates the universe, we can say that the blueprint of the universe is comprised of these 613 parts.

We have access to each one of these parts through the *mitzvah* that specifically relates to it. Consequently, we can influence the entire universe by knowing which particular *mitzvah* is linked to which particular part of the *Sefiroth*. Undoubtedly the modern technological invention of the hologram provides a good model for this process: in a hologram, each part contains all the others.

Thus we can understand the *mitzvoth* as points of binding, or better, as opportunities. Through the Jewish path, we are given 613 different opportunities to draw closer to God; we can take advantage of as many of these as we wish. The more *mitzvoth* we do, the closer we will get to the divine. Each *mitzvah* has the ability to rectify something else in the world; if we were able to perform all of them we would rectify the entire world.

So let us examine how the *mitzvoth* or laws—or binding points—in the Torah are delineated. First, they are traditionally delineated into two basic kinds: the ethical laws and the ritual laws. Some of the 613 fall into one category, some into the other. What is the most important of all the laws? Could we take just one of all the 613 and identify it as the most important? There is a time-honored *midrash* ("folktale") about this. It goes as follows:

> One day a non-Jew sought to find out what the whole Torah was all about. He went to many prominent rabbis of his time and said to each one, 'Look, I don't have much time. Can you tell me quickly what the Torah is all about?' According to the tale, he wanted to know in as short a period as he was able to stand on one foot. Each rabbi sent him away and the man became increasingly intent on an answer to his question. Finally, one rabbi told him, 'The most basic law is: Love thy neighbor as thyself. The rest is commentary. Go and learn.'

So there we have the most fundamental of the 613 laws and it relates to our involvement with one another, between one human being and another. This is because the physical plane is the crucial one in our existence; the connections all occur on the physical plane. Therefore, "Love thy neighbor as thyself" is the most basic law in Judaism; if you wanted to sum up the most fundamental precept of all the 613, that would do it.

Now, more specifically, what are the ethical laws? These, as Maimonides pointed out, are quite easy for all sensitive people to comprehend. They constitute the laws within Judaism such as, "Thou shall not murder," "Don't steal," "Don't tell lies," and so on. Generally, Western culture has accepted and adopted these laws. They are logical and reasonable; we would certainly regard them as necessities for building a just society. We would not really think to question them.

However, the ritual laws are very different. They are much more difficult to comprehend. Indeed, some seem virtually incomprehensible to us today. They appear to make little sense at all. But remember, the ritual laws are ways also of drawing closer to God, and therefore, they encompass a kind of translogic that may be beyond our ability to understand. Sometimes, the sages have provided a rationalization or a logical explanation for the importance of a specific ritual law. But we have been advised for millennia not to accept the ritual law on the basis of the rationalization. Rather, we are commanded to observe the ritual laws simply "because God said so".

Nonetheless, this injunction is not intended to stop us from finding logical reasons for the ritual laws, for such rationalizations often make it easier for us to carry them out. With these concepts in mind, let us now turn to some specific ritual laws and their mystical interpretation.

Tefillen (Phylacteries)

The ritual law in Judaism pertains to those rules that are less incomprehensible and therefore more mysterious. In this chapter we will take a look at several features of Jewish ritual law. Our first example is the *tefillin*. What are they? The written Torah, the Bible, says only, "Bind them to your hands and to your head." Bind what? It says nothing about this. But the oral Torah deals quite specifically with *tefillin*. In fact, this is a good example of how the two Torahs complement one another within Judaism.

For thousands of years, Jews have known exactly what to do with *tefillin* because they saw their fathers use them, and they in turn saw their own fathers use them, and so on backward in time to Moses. Now the *tefillin* are comprised of two leather boxes. Inside each is a handwritten scroll; it is written in a very special way and records a specific section of the Torah. One box goes on the arm and has a leather strap to bind it there. The boxes are always black, made of one piece of leather. There are very strict rules governing their construction. The second box is bound to the head. Because it goes around the head it has a different leather strap, but it too is comprised of one piece of leather. The box that goes on the head actually consists of four sections, four separate scrolls, each one in its own compartment. Each separate scroll contains another specific section of the Torah written by hand.

The *tefillin* are involved in a very strange ritual. Traditionally, Jewish men perform it though there is no prohibition against women doing it, too. We are told that the leather boxes must be constructed in a certain way, and that we have to do a "weird" thing with them: tie one around the hand a prescribed number of times, then tie one around the head a prescribed number of times. The tyings must be done in a prescribed way. There are a whole set of rules concerning the use of these little boxes. What kind of sense can we make of this ritual?

Some analogies to modern scientific knowledge can be helpful in this context. There are all sorts of radio waves bombarding the room in which we sit. In a large city, there may be twenty or thirty radio stations emitting signals that travel through the room. The signals are ultimately information. But unless we have a working radio, plugged into a working socket or using working batteries, we will hear absolutely nothing. We need a radio receiver, a physical apparatus that will take these radio waves and translate them into sounds that we can hear and understand. Bear in mind: the radio does not create the waves but only amplifies them so that we can hear the station.

In a similar way, just as radio waves are traveling now through our rooms and yet depend on a physical apparatus to translate them, so too are there spiritual radio waves traveling to us from a spiritual radio station. These waves are right now in our rooms. They have always been there and they will always be there. If we could translate them somehow into a comprehensible form, then they could be of direct benefit to us. In a like manner, this is how Kabbalists view the *tefillin*. They are constructed in such a way that they are tuned into a particular spiritual radio station and translate that information. The *tefillin* cause the human body to become a receptor for these spiritual energies.

Let us continue the analogy. The Torah relates many laws concerning the construction of *tefillin*. But consider a regular radio for a moment. If we disconnect a single wire or move a single tube or transpose two tubes, the radio will not work one iota. It must be built to very precise specifications. We have to say, "The green wire must go to this knob." We cannot decide to put the green wire where we feel it is more esthetic; nor can we place the tube where we prefer it. The components must go exactly in their proper slots. The same principle holds true for the *tefillin*. That is why the Jewish laws governing them have for millennia been so detailed and exacting.

Of course, once we have a plan for building a radio, it becomes possible for a person who knows nothing about physics to build one. Think of Japan, where millions of working people produce very advanced technology for the world without possessing the vaguest idea of electronic engineering. They simply carry out the blueprint on their factory assembly lines. The same principle holds true for the *tefillin*. Once given a blueprint for their construction, a person could put them together without possessing an understanding of their way of functioning.

To continue the radio analogy, the radio is a very complex piece of equipment if one really wishes to understand it. A full understanding requires substantial knowledge of physics, mathematics, electronics, and other fields. Yet the operation of a radio is extremely simple. Even a two-year-old can learn to turn it on and off.

This also holds true for the *tefillin*. To fully understand their laws would undoubtedly be at least as difficult as to understand the laws that govern a radio receiver. Nevertheless, the use and operation of *tefillin* are so simple that even a child can do it.

In departing from this somewhat detailed analogy, it is important to realize that we are simply seeking ways to understand the Kabbalah in our scientific age. Such scientific analogies seem easier for us to grasp today than some of those rituals of the past, when a theological vocabulary was more accessible to us.

There is a second point to keep in mind concerning the *tefillin*. It can best be illustrated through an intriguing tale about Elijah, the *Gaon* ("Genius") of Vilna (1720-1797). He was renowned throughout the Jewish world as the greatest intellect and scholar of his time. The story goes like this:

> One day, the *Gaon* of Vilna was praying with many of his students in a town in Eastern Europe. They were all in a hotel, praying together. This was a time when pogroms against the Jews were all too commonplace. Suddenly some Russian soldiers approached the hotel. All the students therefore ran away from the hotel as fast as they could to hide in the nearby woods outside the village. When they safely reached the woods, they realized with horror that they had forgotten their teacher in the hotel room. Apparently the *Gaon* had been so immersed in his prayers that he had failed to notice his students' hasty exit.
>
> The students were paralyzed with fear because the old man had been left to fend for himself against the blood-

thirsty soldiers. Nevertheless, they knew that to return to the hotel might only seal their own doom as well. In horror, they waited in the woods. Suddenly, the hotel door was thrown open and they saw the soldiers fleeing in panic away from the hotel and looked inside. There the *Gaon* was still standing and praying. He was in the exact position they had left him.

The students waited for their master to conclude his prayers and then asked him, 'What happened?' Surprised, he looked at them and said, 'What do you mean?' Almost in disbelief, they replied, 'But the soldiers there. . .' The *Gaon* smiled and answered, 'Do you not know that I had my *tefillin* on? When you have your *tefillin* on, you are totally invincible and no power on earth can harm you.' The students were bewildered. Was the *Gaon* serious? And yet, they had just witnessed the burly soldiers running in panic from the hotel.

Several weeks passed. Shmuel, a young student of the *Gaon*'s, was by himself in the woods. He stopped to say his afternoon prayers and put on his *tefillin*. Suddenly he saw some soldiers approaching in the distance. Ordinarily, Shmuel would have fled immediately to hide. But now he knew that he possessed a powerful weapon and no longer needed refuge from any force on earth. Therefore, Shmuel just stood there until the soldiers were almost upon him. And, as he continued to stand, the soldiers proceeded to beat him severely and left him for dead.

Somehow, Shmuel managed to survive the brutal beating and crawl back to the village outskirts, where he was found and helped to recover from his ordeal. A long time later, he made his way back to the *Gaon* and said to him, 'What did you do to me?' The rabbi asked, 'What do you mean, what did I do to you?' Shmuel retorted, 'You told me that if I had these *tefillin* on, then I would be invincible, that no power on earth could harm me. And I believed you and look what happened to me.' He then proceeded to recount how he had been standing alone in the woods, when the soldiers approached and they nearly beat him to death.

When Shmuel finished his story, the *Gaon* smiled gently. 'You misunderstood me,' he commented. 'What happened is that I was talking about the *tefillin* to your group and said *b'rosh* and you thought I was referring to the head *tefillin*— that if you have on the *tefillin* of the head, then you are invincible.' Shmuel nodded. 'Well,' the *Gaon* continued, 'There are two sets of *tefillin*. One set is outside your head and the other lies inside. You put on the outside pair and then you activate the inner set. When the two are working together in unison, then you possess the power.'

Therefore, Kabbalists teach that the ritual of placing the *tefillin* on the head is necessary but not sufficient to generate spiritual strength. It is vital for us to have the awareness of what we are doing in the ritual. In that way, we can activate the internal process that then becomes linked to the external *tefillin*. Analogously, think of a radio that is not plugged into a wall socket. If it remains unplugged, then we can easily be forced to ask, "How come everyone is talking about all this great music that comes from this radio, but I don't hear anything at all?" The radio receiver can be turned on, but it must also be plugged in. Likewise, the electrical current and the electricity may be properly flowing, but these are useless without the radio receiver. It is the mutual collaboration of the electricity and the radio, of the external *tefillin* and the inner set, that somehow cause the life force to awaken.

Many folktales of Judaism and other traditions embody universal truths. One reason that certain folktales retain their allure from generation to generation is precisely that they speak to something timeless in the human condition. The truth can be told in many different versions; therefore, we see the same basic tales offered by various cultures. In our own time, psychoanalysts such as Bruno Bettelheim have highlighted the wisdom that classic fairytales offer men and women throughout the ages. In a way, the biblical narratives exemplify this principle. They contain aspects of inner truth that even children can benefit from hearing; yet, as children mature and become more perceptive they can continue to experience new insights from the biblical accounts. One can begin to penetrate each successive layer or "veil" of the Bible until its most recondite meanings are revealed.

The Mezuzah

The Jewish tradition has for thousands of years incorporated something called a *mezuzah*, which comes in many different shapes. They are also boxes and within each *mezuzah* or box is a scroll. On the scroll is a handwritten portion of the Torah, different from those in the *tefillin*. The *mezuzah* is to be put on the doorposts of houses. Why? Think of our earlier analogy and extend it. Just as people put up a lightning rod on a house, Jews are commanded to put these on the doors. Or, to use another analogy, science has provided us with devices like negative ion generators or air-purifiers, to improve the physical atmosphere of the home. On a spiritual level, a similar kind of situation exists. You can think of the *mezuzoth* as spiritual, negative ion generators. When put on a house, they create a type of receptivity within the house for the incoming spiritual energy. Putting the *mezuzah* there is a necessary requirement for higher awareness, but in itself it is not sufficient. It helps to create the channel.

The same principle is at work if I place a radio in my room but do not plug it in—or I buy a telephone but have not yet connected it to the line. The devices would simply not work. So, too, these ritual objects are necessary but not sufficient for binding ourselves to *Ain Sof* through the ritual laws.

The Ritual Importance of Food

We have earlier mentioned that there were ten sayings, "And God said", that went into the creating of the universe. If we turn to the first chapter of Genesis, we can see what each of these sayings was. The tenth one has to do with food. It was God saying that He was going to make food available to humanity; thus, the tenth saying generated our ability to receive food. Kabbalistically, there is something very special about this ability. The notion is that somehow our spiritual nourishment can take place alongside our physical nourishment, as we consume food. Kabbalists explain that just as the breakdown of food within our body releases physical energy, so too does the eating of food release spiritual energy. Food can be used to nourish our soul.

For this reason, we are instructed to always make a blessing over food before we eat it. We must never place anything in our mouth without first making a blessing over it. This is because if we are engaged in a spiritual act, then there should be spirituality present in what we bring to the act. The same concept pertains to *tefillin*; we must bring a certain consciousness to it, too. Likewise, the *mezuzah* on the doorpost and the *tallis* ("prayer-shawl") which we pray in must be connected to a certain quality within us.

Food contains something spiritual as well as physical. However, to really unleash that spiritual power, to truly use it, we must bring something to it. That something is an awareness of the spiritual aspects within the food—and taking out a moment to say a prayer or blessing over the food. Kabbalists indicate that when we are about to eat the food, we should have the awareness that God is manifesting His creative power for our benefit. When we taste the food, we should realize that God put the taste there. In this way, eating becomes a sacred act that helps maintain our awareness of God.

As a general rule, the Kabbalah teaches that all pleasure on the physical plane really comes from the spiritual factor that infuses the physical object. Whenever one enjoys physical pleasure, he or she should therefore realize that the pleasure really comes from the spiritual component of that physical thing. This involves taking time to appreciate that every source of pleasure is ultimately spiritual in nature. That is why Judaism has many ritual laws related to physical pleasure—taking a moment out from daily routine to just say a blessing, or to make the act more than just physical.

Of course, the topic of food brings us to the whole range of dietary laws within Judaism. Some specific foods are forbidden to Jews; others must not be eaten in certain combinations. These laws have nothing to do with our physical health; they relate to our spiritual health. Let us take one example: pork. It is one of the forbidden foods in Judaism. Interestingly, the Hebrew word pork has "return" as its root. Why is this so? Kabbalists explain that there is nothing about pork that is bad or evil per se; there will come a time when pork will return to being something that Jews can eat. There will come a time when pork will return to the same level of holiness that other foods possess. The point is that the exclusion of certain foods in Judaism is not meant in any way to demean these or to suggest that they are bad for human health. Of course, these foods are not at all banned to those who follow a non-Jewish spiritual path; they are only forbidden to people who follow the Jewish path.

Sacred Time

There is yet another intriguing facet of ritual from the Kabbalistic perspective: the holidays throughout the Jewish year. Without dwelling on particular holidays, I would like to set forth the basic Kabbalistic principle about these. There is an interesting analogy that can make this principle clear and it relates to our space program.

When the government wants to send a rocket to the moon, scientists speak of what they call "windows". These refer to certain times when the rocket can be sent up. A "window" is the alignment of the planets and all the other forces. On those days of the year when an "open window" exists, conditions are most advantageous for launching the rocket. Of course, the earth's local weather must be right, too.

Keep this idea in mind when you think of the Jewish holidays. There are certain times when a rocket can be sent up, and certain times when it cannot be sent. This is because on the days when those windows are closed, the chance of success is quite limited. If the scientists really want the launch to succeed, they must take advantage of what they know about the gravitational and other forces that govern the universe. They must know that there are special times—open windows—when the launch will be most likely to succeed. This notion is very much akin to the Jewish concept of holidays.

To Kabbalists, the holiday is not an arbitrary day. Even if the holiday commemorates an event that took place in history, such as Passover, the holiday when the Jews left their bondage in Egypt, that event occurred on the particular day for a reason. Just as there are physical windows that open at certain times of the year, so too are there spiritual windows. These latter windows relate to the heavenly bodies, which Kabbalists view as connecting spiritual forces to earthly existence.

From this perspective, the Jewish holidays correspond to spiritual "open windows", when it is possible for spiritual events to occur more easily. That is why a particular miracle happened on a particular day or time of the year. Every time in the yearly cycle that the same day reoccurs, the same events are made available to us. We can contact the same forces that brought about those miracles on those specific days.

For this reason, Kabbalists see the various prayers, meditations, and rituals that surround each holiday as definite techniques for taking advantage of the window that is open on that particular day or time of the year.

The Sabbath

There is one special window that comes more often than once per year and that, of course, is the Sabbath. It is a very special window that comes once per week in the cycle of events. What is its mystical significance? Throughout the centuries of Judaism, observance of the Sabbath has probably been the most outstanding ritual. There is even an ancient statement of the sages that, "As much as the Jews have kept the Sabbath, the Sabbath has kept the Jews." The notion is that the entire integrity of Judaism has been maintained through the ritual observance of the Sabbath.

To emphasize this point, it is helpful to know that the Sabbath is the only ritual to be mentioned in the Ten Commandments. It is the Fourth Commandment. Also, the laws concerning the Sabbath are repeated in the Torah more often than any other laws. Some ritual laws in the Torah are indeed repeated, but the Sabbath law is repeated more frequently than any other. The Talmudic sages equated violation of the Sabbath to the worshipping of idols; they even considered desecration of the Sabbath as a capital offense.

What is so important about the Sabbath? The popular explanation today is that it marks a day of rest. That is a pleasant idea, but hardly one possessing spiritual urgency. Kabbalists suggest, though, that one look at the Ten Commandments. The first three all relate to God. The First establishes that there is a God. The Second speaks of God's unity. The Third tells us to respect God. And the Fourth, right after the three that relate to God's existence, God's unity, and God's respect, pertains to the Sabbath.

The Bible recounts that on the seventh day God rested. But what does this really mean? Was God tired? Creating the universe in six days might be hard work for most of us, but we would not necessarily conclude that it would tire out God, so that He needed to rest on that day.

If one reads Genesis 2:2, one will see that it says something very interesting: "God finished his work on the seventh day." Does this statement not hold an apparent contradiction? If it took God six days to create the universe, then what did

He finish on the seventh day? Something must have happened on the seventh day, or else the Bible would indicate that God finished creation on the sixth day. Kabbalists teach that God created rest on the seventh day; in six days, He created all this work and on the seventh day, He created rest.

What does "rest" mean in God's terms? Kabbalists explain that He stopped creating; He no longer interfered with the world. Remember, the one thing that we have said about God is that He is unchanging; God's nature is to not change. The specific biblical reference for this is Malachi 3:6, "I am God, I do not change." So, if God does not change and yet so many changes occur in the six days of Creation, then the seventh day represents a day of harmony between God's true nature and the universe. It is a day in which change no longer occurs and when the cosmos is in harmony with God.

On this theme, the *Zohar* ("Book of Splendor"), a key text of the Kabbalah, relates that on the seventh day God created harmony between Himself and the universe because He created rest, nonchange. So too, when man participates in the Sabbath observance, he or she is not to inflict any change on the universe. Rather, the goal is to achieve a state of harmony between ourselves and the cosmos, as much as God set the example on that day to not change anything at all.

This observance is a primary Jewish example of how to emulate God. Other Jewish laws involve obeying God. In contrast, to have one day when the creative process altogether ceases is a prime example of emulating God, of doing as God does. The Sabbath is a day when instead of seeking to change the world, we journey inward and spend time within our selves. We emulate God by relinquishing our mastery over the world on the Sabbath Day.

The Kabbalistic definition of "rest", therefore, is not necessarily to lounge in a chair. The definition of rest as used in the Bible means not interfering with nature and not exhibiting any mastery over it. It is a day of peace between man and nature. Thus, the Sabbath laws do not really pertain so much to mere physical labor as to acts of mastery over nature. Plucking a rose or lighting a match involve very little physical labor, certainly less than such permitted Sabbath acts as conversing, reading, or eating. But to pluck a rose or light a match involves mastery over nature.

The Talmud comments that the Messianic Age will be an era in which a total Sabbath will reign all the time. That is, total harmony between man and the universe will exist. Thus, the Sabbath is a way to remind us of our ultimate purpose in life: to serve the Holy One. Once a week the Sabbath day recalls for us the existence of a higher reality than the mundane.

The Kabbalah also teaches that we receive an additional aspect to our souls on the Sabbath because, in a sense, that is one way to understand the nature of this special "open window". It is easier on that day to get the spiritual rocket to the moon. It is easier to make the connection then, for on that day the universal, spiritual forces are more advantageously aligned for us. Therefore the Sabbath marks the weekly opening of a very special window.

What is also intriguing about the Sabbath is that in order to fulfill its observance, one does not have to *do* anything. It is in the abstaining of doing that one fulfills the law, not in the doing. Even if you sleep the whole Sabbath day, you can fulfill the commandment. All you have to do is to not do; on that day God will do the rest. Think of it in this way: all week long you struggle to reach a certain spiritual level. But on this day, you need not struggle at all. On this day, if you simply refrain from doing, God will come down and make this connection the rest of the way. From this perspective, the Sabbath is a very sacred and meaningful day. Its observance marks a very special ritual law and holds a central place within the Kabbalistic or Torah path.

Sacred Places

Since we have mentioned the holidays and Sabbath as special times, it is also important to note that the Kabbalah speaks of special places as well. Just as there are places on the earth like the North Pole, where the magnetic forces are stronger than elsewhere, analogously there are places on earth where the spiritual forces are more powerful. There are several of these special places and they are where certain miracles have occurred. Kabbalists stress that the place did not become holy because a miracle occurred there; rather, the miracle happened there because that was a special place to begin with. The prime Kabbalistic example of a special place is the site of Jerusalem. For millennia, Jews have regarded it as a gateway to holiness on the physical plane. Spiritual growth is seen to be easier for us at that sacred place.

Prayer

Let us briefly turn to the Kabbalistic concept of prayer. Today many people are very confused about the nature of prayer. It occupies a central position in the Torah path because there are a specific number of times each day that a male Jew is obliged to pray; each individual male must say these prayers. But most people nowadays are very unclear about what prayer is all about.

Many people approach the act of praying to God from the viewpoint of asking or begging God for something; we plead with Him to give us something we want and need. This is how we conceive of prayer. The Kabbalistic perspective is very different. Kabbalists insist that we do not have to ask God for anything. God already knows what we want, for it is impossible that He did not know before we asked Him. Kabbalists further say that as much as we may want something, God wants even more to give it to us.

A good analogy for this involves a parent and child. The child may really want something—say, a tasty food that has been prepared. The parent knows that giving the food to the child will make him happy; and the parent may experience even more intense pleasure giving the food than the child experiences while eating it. To Kabbalists, God is like this good parent. He wants to give the desired object to us; He is eager to give it. Prayer is not needed to beg or persuade God to give it to us, for God is unchangeable; we cannot "change God's mind".

Rather, the whole purpose of prayer is to change ourselves, not God. All that we must do is make ourselves worthy of God's gift. Prayer is a way of making ourselves more deserving of that which we want. It has nothing to do with God, in the sense that God might change through our act of prayer. Through prayer, we have the opportunity to alter ourselves, to raise our consciousness to a much higher spiritual level. One might ask, though: why do Jews repeat the same prayers over and over? The answer is that the prayers are specific *mantras*—very specific spiritual clues. We might recall here our discussion of the Hebrew alphabet and the combination of these words and letters. All that information was encoded in the traditional prayers—in the ritual prayers—when prophecy ceased. There were a thousand years of prophecy, from the time of Moses' revelation until the last prophet of Israel. The prophets knew that there would be a time of spiritual "famine" when this divine prophecy ended. The last surviving prophets, together with the other sages of their day, decided that the Jewish people would need something to help guide them in the absence of prophecy. Therefore they encoded in the ritual prayers all the necessary information to reach more exalted spiritual levels.

Of course, individuals can make rituals into dessicated things. They can become very mechanical about performing religious rituals. This seems to be a common phenomenon with all religions, and Judaism is no exception. But Kabbalists would say that even if one simply repeats the Hebrew words without any higher awareness, there is still a very strong spiritual connection present. The ideal is to develop the sensitivity to the more hidden and powerful forces inherent in the ritual prayers.

In this context, the English translation of the ritual prayers does not seem to help many people. For example, many prayers begin in this way: "Blessed are You, God . . ."—as in the prayer over food: "Blessed are You, God, O King of the universe, Who created the fruit of the tree." This sort of translation is really quite silly: it suggests that we are going to bless God. However, the Kabbalistic notion is that prayer is intended neither to bless nor to thank God. Its purpose is to elevate our own consciousness.

Teshuvah (Repentance)

Another basic concept is that of repentance—repenting for not following the sacred path. The Hebrew word for this notion is *teshuvah*, which literally means "to return". Kabbalists therefore teach that repentance is a way of returning to the Source, of coming home again. They also emphasize that one who repents is at a higher spiritual level than one who never sinned in the first place. For many people, this concept is rather puzzling. They feel that it really is not fair. If I have not been sinning all the time and have been following the divine path properly, why is it that I can only reach one level, whereas someone else, who had been committing many sins and then repented can achieve a higher level? The answer is that if someone has never been tempted to stray from the straight and narrow, he or she really has not accomplished that much. Those people who have truly tasted temptation and have overcome such impulses within have accomplished much more. One who is involved in sinfulness or evil and has overcome such forces is definitely at a higher level than one who has never been involved. The involvement does not necessarily have to mean actively going out and doing evil; but it really has to involve a recognition of the evil within.

This principle is certainly psychologically true. Many of us who are involved with a psychological path know that to really be able to deal with hate and anger in others, we must be able to see the hatefulness and anger within ourselves. If one goes through life and has never hated anyone and has never become angry toward anyone, what kind of saint is he? It is only when one has truly tasted the anger within himself—and then overcome it—that he has finally reached a point of psychological maturity. To have never been angry and never tasted it—that is not psychological maturity.

The same principle is valid spiritually. Certainly I am hardly suggesting that we go out, commit many sins, and then repent. But the idea is that we must understand the sinfulness within us and be able to deal with it. This is because if we do not come to grips with that, we may still reach a righteous level—but we will never attain real inner heights.

A long-standing Kabbalistic dictum on *teshuvah* is that it was created before the world itself. What does this mean? It means that *teshuvah* is outside the realm of time and unbounded by time. One can go back, one can return. The fact that one did something a year ago or yesterday is immaterial. True enough, in the physical world one cannot go back; one cannot undo what has already been done. But if *teshuvah* exists outside of time, then one can go back and undo what has been done spiritually. The undoing of the sin comes when the knowledge of the sin is transformed into a longing for good. Then the sin becomes a divine force.

This Kabbalistic concept is akin to our earlier story of the gardener in the king's palace. The gardener longs to do good and this longing comes from the fact that he knows that he acted wrongly. Therefore the force that drove him to do bad in the first place has been converted into a striving force to do good: through his striving, rectification takes place.

Let us now try a very useful meditation based on *teshuvah*. Let us think back over the course of our lives to date and visualize the worst sin that we have ever committed. Let us imagine that sin and then think about how we feel about our act now, from the perspective of this moment. That is, we should travel back in time and mentally recommit the sin— but commit it again with our current awareness, rather than the attitude we originally possessed.

When we can truly do this, we will feel a change within ourselves. And when we feel this inner change, then we can turn to God. In a sense, it is like admitting that we did this and are asking for forgiveness. We can imagine that God, who created *teshuvah* outside of time, has taken the sin itself and has made it cease to exist. All that is left is our motive of going back in time to change it. Only the thought of how we feel about it now continues to exist. If we do this, we can feel a burden lifted from ourselves.

A relevant question can be posed concerning this technique. What if we feel that our sin has upset someone else's life and that we cannot undo its harmful effect—for example, death from a murder. We cannot go back in time and bring the person back to life again. Kabbalists answer this question by saying that on the physical level we cannot go back in time, but on the spiritual level we can. Of course, they also make a distinction between sins against God—which are more what this exercise involves—and sins against other people. Sins that we commit against others usually must be rectified on a physical as well as spiritual level. As an aside, one might add that the Jewish Day of Atonement, Yom Kippur, provides a special open "window" when *teshuvah* is possible to a greater degree than at any other time during the year.

Magic and Applied Kabbalah

The Kabbalistic view of what we today might call "magic" or "miracles" is really based on the notion that God decreed during Creation that the laws of nature should not be absolute, but changeable. It points to several sources of such magic. One source relates to the Names of God. The Kabbalah teaches that when certain Names of God are used to call Him, one has access to spiritual influence associated with the Names.

THE THREE VERSES IN HEBREW*

וַיִּסַּע מַלְאַךְ הָאֱלֹהִים הַהֹלֵךְ לִפְנֵי מַחֲנֵה יִשְׂרָאֵל וַיֵּלֶךְ מֵאַחֲרֵיהֶם וַיִּסַּע עַמּוּד
הֶעָנָן מִפְּנֵיהֶם וַיַּעֲמֹד מֵאַחֲרֵיהֶם:

וַיָּבֹא בֵּין ׀ מַחֲנֵה מִצְרַיִם וּבֵין מַחֲנֵה יִשְׂרָאֵל וַיְהִי הֶעָנָן וְהַחֹשֶׁךְ וַיָּאֶר אֶת־
הַלָּיְלָה וְלֹא־קָרַב זֶה אֶל־זֶה כָּל־הַלָּיְלָה:

וַיֵּט מֹשֶׁה אֶת־יָדוֹ עַל־הַיָּם וַיּוֹלֶךְ ׀ יְהוָה ׀ אֶת־הַיָּם בְּרוּחַ קָדִים עַזָּה כָּל־
הַלַּיְלָה וַיָּשֶׂם אֶת־הַיָּם לֶחָרָבָה וַיִּבָּקְעוּ הַמָּיִם:

THE SEVENTY-TWO TRIPLETS

כהת	אבא	ללה	מהש	עלם	סיט	ילי	והו
הקם	הרי	מבה	יזל	ההע	לאו	אלד	הזי
חרו	מלה	ייי	נלך	פהל	לוו	כלי	לאו
ושר	לכב	אום	ריי	שאה	ירת	האא	נתה
ייז	רהע	חעם	אני	מנד	כוק	להח	יחו
מיה	עשל	ערי	סאל	ילה	וול	מיכ	ההה
פוי	מבה	נית	ננא	עמם	החש	דני	והו
מחי	ענו	יהה	ומב	מצר	הרח	ייל	נמם
טום	היי	יבמ	ראה	חבו	איע	מנק	דמב

*Exodus 14: 19, 20, 21

For example, the accompanying diagram contains three consecutive verses from the Bible. Kabbalists have long noticed a very intriguing aspect about these: that each verse contains seventy-two letters. This is the only place in the Bible where this occurs. Now, there is a Name of God that is constituted of seventy-two letters and is known as the "Name of the seventy-two". Kabbalists take these seventy-two letter verses in the Bible and divide them into triplets. Their method is to take the first letter of the first verse, the last letter of the second verse, and the first letter of the third verse; this produces the first triplet. Then they take the second letter of the first verse, the second to last letter of the second verse, and the second letter of the third verse; this generates the next triplet, and so on. Also, there are ways to go backwards and forwards in the arranging of these triplets.

For thousands of years, Kabbalists have taught that with these triplets the leaders of the Jewish people have been able to perform miracles. For instance, it is through these triplets that Moses was able to split the Red Sea. We are told too that Moses—before becoming the Jewish law-giver—killed an Egyptian through the use of these words. There is a very interesting account in the Oral Tradition about this issue.

The *Midrash* relates that Moses grew up as a prince in the Pharaoh's palace. The Bible itself tells us nothing about Moses' youth. It simply states that one day when he was already a grown man—in his thirties or forties, depending on the particular version of the *Midrash*—he went outside and saw an Egyptian beating a Jew. Moses intervened, killed the Egyptian, then buried him.

The next time that Moses traveled outside the palace, he saw two Jews who were fighting. He stepped between them and tried to break up their conflict. They said to him, "Look, who told you that you are in charge of us? Are you going to kill us the way you did that Egyptian?" Immediately Moses ran away from Egypt.

This is a very puzzling episode. Why would Moses have to run away? True, he killed someone, but this was a culture in which he, a prince, had killed a rather low-level individual. So why should Moses have been worried? Why couldn't he— as an Egyptian prince—kill whomever he wanted? Why was

Moses suddenly so terrified that Pharaoh would kill him for murdering an Egyptian? Kabbalists explain this matter by indicating that Moses was not really worried over his act of killing the Egyptian. Rather, Moses was concerned about how he had committed this act. Moses did not hit the man with his fists, but had uttered one of these words and thereby used spiritual force. Once Moses had used that force, he had revealed himself; he had revealed that he knew Kabbalistic magic and that he was in essence a Jew. And not only was he a Jew, but he possessed this great power. This situation would certainly have posed a dire threat to Pharaoh. Therefore, when Moses learned that others knew what he had done, he had to flee—for now Pharaoh would know who he really was.

Let us recall the biblical account of Moses' birth. Pharaoh had received a prophecy that a child would be born to the Hebrew slaves who would lead them out of bondage. Pharaoh immediately tried to kill all the male children born that year, because he knew that this special child would be born in that period. The infant Moses, though, was secreted and therefore escaped. The Pharaoh would now realize that this special child had grown up in the royal palace and possessed great power.

We are told that Moses' mother initially hid him for as long as she could. When hiding him was no longer possible, then she placed him in a small boat where he was thereupon discovered by the Pharaoh's daughter. Moses' sister Miriam, who was watching the boat to see what would happen to the infant, came up to the princess and asked her if she wished a helper to nurse it. The princess assented and took the infant Moses back to his mother. Consequently, with the blessing of the princess, Moses was raised by his own mother and spent an unknown amount of time with her before he was brought back to the royal palace.

Interestingly, the Kabbalah also teaches that this particular daughter of Pharaoh had already converted to Judaism before she discovered Moses. Indeed, this conversion was part of the chain of events. She had converted to Judaism and was actually going to bathe in the river—for this was the *mikvah* ceremony of conversion. At that moment she found the infant Moses, and experienced this divine synchronicity as an answer to her prayer and confirmation that she was acting correctly. Thus, not only was Moses originally raised by his own biological mother—who nursed him through his formative years—but he was raised in the royal palace by the Pharaoh's daughter, who herself had become a Jew. Undoubtedly she helped to enhance Moses' education.

When Moses realized that the two fighting Jews had seen him kill the Egyptian through mystical means, then he knew that his "cover was blown". But why did Moses not simply kill these two if they posed a dangerous threat to his mission? The answer is that Moses was not yet ordained by God to do anything; he had killed the Egyptian acting on his own impulses. It was only some forty years later—when Moses was eighty years old—when he encountered God in the Burning Bush. It was only after many decades of spiritual growth that he arrived at a point lofty enough to have developed his powers. At that point, he knew enough to do the magic, so to speak, but he was hardly at that level when he killed the Egyptian. It would take another forty or fifty years of inner ascent before he would experience the Burning Bush.

To summarize, the Names of God can transmit spiritual forces under certain conditions. But it is not simply a matter of knowing which Name to utter. Unless one knows the conditions under which the Name is to be used, then the Name itself is meaningless. It is similar to our description of the *tefillin*; both parts of the "equation" are necessary for true power.

Another Kabbalistic technique of magic relates to the use of angels. Kabbalists have long taught that there are ways to coerce angels to do certain things. You can be a very righteous person, one very close to God, and through that closeness you can acquire influence over angels and bid them to use their powers to do what you want. However, you can also influence angels without being a righteous individual at all. You simply follow various procedures—as in using any tool—and then literally coerce angels to do certain acts. But you must be very careful when doing that, because the angels might try to get back at you later. Therefore, you have to know what you are doing. Nevertheless, the fact exists that it is possible to coerce angels by knowing how the spiritual laws work and the rules by which angels work. Since man has the ability to see beyond an angel, he can coerce angels into doing things. Demons (*Shedim* in Hebrew) are part of magic, too. They are beings that exist in between the physical and the spiritual realms. Kabbalists consider them "forces"—transitory between physical and spiritual. There is a whole system within the Kabbalah for how to make these demons act as you bid them to. However, these forces all have certain limitations: they can only do things over which they have power.

Now, in the same way that we have discussed linking a spiritual thing to something physical—so, too, can we link spiritual forces to a name. This is because Kabbalists view a name as something physical; it can be written down. This approach becomes the basis for charms and amulets and other ritualistic, magical objects long associated with the Kabbalah. Adepts have taught that it is possible to bind certain forces to a physical object; then that physical object becomes a focus for the transmission of that particular spiritual power. Bear in mind, though, that such magical techniques are seen to have little if anything to do with our spiritual growth. We can unquestionably perfect ourselves spiritually without ever touching any of the forces of magic, though these can be used. All the prophets most certainly used them, as did Moses himself.

THE MESSIAH

We come now to Kabbalistic teaching about the Messiah. Here, we must look at the Jewish concept in relation to the Christian notion. First, the Hebrew term is *Moschiach*— literally, "the anointed one, the one who is anointed". In biblical days, the prophets would anoint special individuals, such as one who was to be king. The Hebrew king was always anointed by a prophet. Therefore, Jewish tradition has it that the *Moschiach* is to be like a king and is to be anointed by a prophet.

Another way to look at this idea is that the Messiah is a messenger. His function is to raise humanity's consciousness to bring about universal peace. What does the Kabbalah tell us about the Messiah and his time of coming? The classic teaching is that there are two separate but related ways in which the Messiah can come. The first way is that the Messiah can come at any time in history, if people are truly observing the path of God. However, if humanity does not choose to obey God's laws, then time will run out. If that possibility occurs, the Messiah will come at the end of a certain period of time.

In other words, the Holy One decreed that there would be a six thousand year period of history in this earthly cycle. During this epoch, humanity would have an opportunity to establish harmony and justice. Any time that the people of the world accomplished this, the Messiah would come and bring the Messianic Age of total peace and unity. But if the six thousands years elapsed and nothing happened to bring the Messiah, then the Messiah would come because time had run out.

Now, Jewish mystics teach that there will be definite consequences if the Messiah must come in this second way. To make matters clearer, it is helpful to know the Kabbalistic view that in every generation of this six thousand year epoch, there is at least one person who can serve as the Messiah. There is always one or more individuals who can assume that special mantle of leadership if the world is ready for that. If not, then in every generation, the potential Messiah must die and the generation will die with him. Yet the next generation has its own potential Messiah. And so, every generation has its specific potential Messiah from the beginning of our cycle to its final day.

The second way for the Messiah to come is not very pleasant. The prophecies say that there will be world destruction, world war. Millions upon millions of men and women will perish. Out of that terrible destruction, the Messiah will emerge as a leader of the surviving remnant.

Kabbalists follow the mainstream Jewish calendar, so now we are in the Year 5747 (1986 in the Roman calendar). There are two reasons why the exact time of the Messiah's coming is not known. First, as just mentioned, he can come at any time that the world has become sufficiently redeemed. Second, because the Hebrew year six thousand will already mark the well-established state of world peace, the Messianic period will already be well in place by then. Thus, if that epoch were already well-established by the year six thousand, then the Messiah must certainly come before that year. An entire chain of events must occur and this may even take two centuries. The Messiah, therefore, will begin a process. He will live and die. His son will reestablish the chain of David, which we have already discussed. This means that even within this countdown period of six thousand years, a couple of hundred years of preparation and transition may be necessary. In this way, planetary harmony will have been achieved by then.

Thus, even within the frame of the countdown, we are very close to something about to occur. By this, Kabbalists suggest that much has to happen before the world war and destruction; that the pre-Messianic period will be one of great change and upheaval. We have already mentioned their view of the current lifting of humanity's curses and other related phenomena. Kabbalists insist then that we are very close to a point of no return. Yet, we can still do something to bring about the Messiah through out efforts for peace and justice. Otherwise, the Messiah will come through the other way.

But how do Kabbalists know that the Messiah has not already come? Certainly there are many people who believe that Jesus was the Messiah and that we await his second return. Why do Kabbalists disagree? There are several important reasons for their position. First is the notion that the Messianic era was never fulfilled. The prophets taught that the Messiah's coming would herald a millennia of peace; there would be no more war, the "lion would lie down with the lamb". The prophets emphatically preached that there would be change in man's very nature. Through the Prophet Isaiah, God promised, "I will give you a new heart." From the Hebrew prophets' view, we would enter into a wholly different relation with one another and with the entire cosmos. Since these prophecies were not realized in Jesus' time, then the primary requisite of the Messiah was not fulfilled.

Christianity for nearly two thousand years has experienced this same problem: that religion is based on what Christians call the Old Testament and the same Hebrew Prophets. Therefore, Christian theologians have taught that their Messiah will come again a second time to bring about these prophecies of the End of Days. But the notion of a "second coming" appears nowhere in the prophets' writings, nowhere in the Bible, nowhere in the Kabbalah. One might argue that Jesus was one of the potential Messiahs in his generation. But one could not argue from the Bible that he was the Messiah. The most one could say, remaining true to the biblical test, is that Jesus could have been the Messiah in his era.

Another reason why Kabbalists reject Jesus as the Messiah is that the prophets clearly speak of the Messiah as a son of man, not as a son of God. The notion of the Messiah as the son of God has no basis in the Bible. The prophets preached quite clearly that the Messiah would be a human being—the son of Adam, in fact—and would live and die, just as all people have done.

The Catholic idea of the immaculate conception raises many objections for Kabbalists, aside from the explanation that Joseph adopted the infant Jesus. This is because the Jewish prophecies teach that the Messiah will be a scion of "the house of David". Actually, this teaching has led to two schools of Christian thought on the identity of Jesus. Some schools trace Joseph back to the house of David. But if Jesus was born of Mary and not of Joseph, how could he be considered a descendant of David? Other scriptures in the New Testament suggest, though, that Mary originated from the house of David, so two versions have long existed.

The whole question of immaculate conception is quite interesting, because it seems to hinge on a mistranslation of a Hebrew word. The Hebrew term is *na'arah*—literally, "a young girl". The prophets preach that a *na'arah* will conceive and give birth to the Messiah. But the Hebrew word does not mean "a virgin". Historically, the Greek translation of the Hebrew Bible somehow mistranslated the word as "virgin". Thus, early Christian thinkers felt compelled to insist that Jesus had been born of a virgin. However, the Hebrew word for "virgin" is *betulah* and nowhere in the prophetic books does it appear.

A third reason why Kabbalists reject Jesus as the Messiah is that the prophets indicate that the Messiah will die and then his son will continue his mission. Obviously this situation did not occur with Jesus. Finally, Kabbalists point to the prophecies that the Messiah will do nothing to alter the Torah as it exists. And, of course, Christianity diverged very sharply from Judaism and its laws of observance. It must be acknowledged, though, that some Christians to this day insist that Jesus never sought to alter the Torah, and that only later did his followers institute the various changes from Jewish to Christian practice. For these reasons, then, Kabbalists—and Jews in general—cannot embrace Jesus as having been the Messiah.

The Messianic Current in History

If the Jews have not accepted Jesus as the Messiah, then who is the Messiah? This question brings us back to the Kabbalistic teaching about Adam. As we have already mentioned, the notion is that human evolution took place over millions of years. Humans evolved from lower to increasingly higher stages. When their evolution reached a certain physical endpoint, then they were ready for the next step: a leap in consciousness and spirituality to the Messianic era.

At that point in time, the Holy One sent a special person to the earth, an individual literally different in species from all other men and women of that time. That individual was Adam. Six thousands years ago, Adam appeared on the global scene. He was the first potential Messiah. That was his role. To be the Messiah means to teach humanity something about the awareness of spiritual growth and the awareness of God. Adam failed in his mission. He therefore lost the capacity to be the Messiah. However, the task of serving as the Messiah remained with his offspring so that there would always be a descendant of his who had this mission.

Now, what happened with Adam's first two children, Cain and Abel? They had the capacity to assume the mission. Abel was killed. Cain, a murderer, certainly could not serve as Adam's successor. The task had not yet been fulfilled. The next event in the biblical narrative is that the "sons of God" mated with the "daughters of men". That is, those of Adam's sacred strain began to intermarry with the humans who came through the long evolutionary process. Adam's unique strain, possessing the gift of prophecy, the gift of longevity, and other wondrous capabilities, therefore became enmeshed in the same mire of sinfulness and physicality that had characterized the "daughters of men". Instead of acting in such a way as to uplift the rest of humanity, the "sons of God" fell into the same morass of lower consciousness.

Exactly ten generations after Adam the biblical account of Noah takes place. God looked at the world and saw that not only had Adam failed in his mission, but that nearly all of Adam's descendants were just as sinful as everyone else. There was almost no difference between the "sons of God" and the "daughters of men". God decided that this situation could no longer continue.

It is then that the great flood occurs. Of course, we know from archaelogical and other evidence that there may have been a catastrophic flood, but that not everybody on the globe was destroyed. The Bible itself—as well as the Talmud—accounts for that. If you read these sacred works closely, you will see that they declare that "the sons of God" were destroyed. This is because the "sons of God", constituting this special strain, were now intermarrying and giving their genetic potential to the rest of humanity. It was in their settlements that the flood surged most strongly. The flood destroyed all the "sons of God" on earth, except for Noah and his children. Noah himself was not quite up to the task of serving as the Messiah. He was merely a little better than the rest of the people around him. Therefore, he was left to survive and to carry on this special strain.

From Noah comes Abraham. Then the Bible presents the narrative about Abraham, often called the first Jew. Abraham was the first of the potential Messiahs of this strain to actually go out into the world and preach the truth of God. In retrospect, he is therefore called the first Jew. But the important point is that he actually placed himself before the public eye and sought to elevate the common level of spirituality by communicating God's laws. Abraham's work was far from complete. However, it was carried out by his son Isaac and by Isaac's son Jacob in the succeeding generation. Jacob, in turn, produced twelve sons. One of them was Joseph, who was sold into slavery in Egypt. Joseph rose from a slave to becoming second only to the Pharaoh; through Joseph's influence, his brothers and his father Jacob came to Egypt.

At this point, though, the Jews were not a nation. They

were really only a family: Jacob and his twelve sons, together with their wives and children. Altogether there were sixty people in this family who came down to Egypt. There they initially prospered, but then became enslaved by a new Pharaoh. There was still no Jewish nation; there was only a family of people who followed the teachings of their great-grandfather Abraham, who taught them about God. This group of people lived in Egypt in slavery until the advent of Moses. Now we have come to Moses in the biblical narrative. Moses exerted his leadership—under God's command—to forge this very large, enslaved, extended family into a nation, a unified people. Kabbalists teach that the whole concept of the unification of the Jewish people is directly related to the nature of the Messiah. That is because at this point in time it was no longer possible for one individual to be the Messiah. It had now become the mission of Adam's children—through Noah and then Abraham, down to Moses. It had now become the task of an entire nation, Israel, to pick up the challenge of the Messianic mantle and carry it.

But if Adam had not sinned, then, in a sense, none of these later events would have been necessary. There would have been no need for "a nation of priests" or the path of Torah. Nor would the *mitzvos* (ritual observances) have been necessary. All of this happened because one man had the capability and failed to actualize it. The people who fled from Egypt then accepted upon themselves this challenge—in order to bring about the redemption of all humanity.

A HOLY PEOPLE

What does the notion of "a holy people" mean? The ancient concept does not really mean that the Jews are better than anyone else. Rather, it means that the Jews possess a responsibility to behave very conscientiously; they must be a "nation of priests". They must be apart from the rest of humanity, in a sense, because their path is much more difficult than that of others. That is, the path of the non-Jews is relatively easy; the path for the Jews has been seen as far harder. For the life of a priest is much more difficult than the life of a lay person. This is true for all religions.

The priest has a special obligation to help others—not just himself—become closer to God. To accomplish this task, the priest must live a much more stringent life than other people. For this reason, the Jews, constituting "a nation of priests", have had to follow a path separate and apart from all others. In this way, the Messianic task may be fulfilled. Kabbalistically, this is who the early Jews were, and why their path was different.

Now, once the Jews were welded into a nation, their path became available to everyone. It was no longer necessary to be born into the Jewish nation to be a Jew; anyone who wished to become a Jew could do so by accepting the challenge of the path. Anyone who wanted to live the life of a "priest" as circumscribed by the Bible, and assume the extra obligations involved, could do so. This fact remains true to the present day.

Judaism has never encouraged proselytizing, though. Indeed, for thousands of years the rabbis have sought to discourage those who wished to become Jews. They have done so because they know how hard the path is. But the discouragement is not intended to suggest that conversion is forbidden or wrong. Anyone who seeks to lead the separate life of the Jews can do so.

For Kabbalists, then, what is the essential difference between the two paths? Certainly, they have taught that we can draw close to God by following a non-Jewish spiritual path. In fact, they have preached that one can become as close to God with a non-Jewish path as he can by following the Jewish path. The difference is simply this: that the Jewish path not only brings its practitioners closer to God, but it brings all of humanity closer to God. This is because the Jewish path is that of the "priest" who acts not only for himself or herself—but for many other people.

Kabbalists therefore insist that one can draw very near to God by following, say, a Buddhist or any other non-Jewish path, but only that individual would be elevated: he or she could not bring others along, too. As has been suggested before, the Jews were obligated to this path. But someone who is not Jewish, and who does not assume the obligations, can draw as close to God as any Jew can. Yet such an individual would bring no others closer to the divine. Only the Jewish path can elevate all of humanity. That is why this path is so much harder than all the others. The path of the priest is that of one who is willing to assume the burden of not only his own salvation, but that of others as well.

Jewish mystics have thus taught that the Messiah will come if enough individuals follow this path as priests. Once a certain "critical mass" of people following the Jewish path exists, then the Messiah can come without any semblance of world destruction or war. But if that "critical mass" is absent, then we will run out of time.

In a sense, we can therefore state that the whole purpose of the Kabbalah is to serve as a way to clarify the path of the priest for his own sake and for the sake of the whole world. In this regard, we have returned to a definition of this ancient system—and in so doing, we have come full circle to our starting point. Early in this book we defined the Kabbalah as meaning "to receive". Now we have discovered what it is that one has received. The Jewish people have received a path—an obligation and a burden—but also the ability to bring about a different world for all humanity. This, then, is the basis and the purpose of the Kabbalistic view of the world and the path it has come to clarify for us.

CHAPTER EIGHT

Meditative Exercises

EXERCISE 1. THE SOUNDS OF CREATION

There are twenty-two letters in the Hebrew alphabet. Traditionally, they have been grouped in various ways. One way is to have double letters, three mother letters, and twelve other kinds of letters. This feature of the Kabbalah is especially germane to the Tree of Life and the relationship of the different *Sefiroth* to one another. Certain letters are linked to other letters in special ways.

The term "mother letters" can be understood to indicate the these are the three basic sounds from which all other sounds emanate. On a phonetic basis, if we have the Hebrew letters *Shin*, *Mem*, and *Aleph*, we have all the sounds. The *Aleph* represents silence, the *Mem* is pure tone, and the *Shin* is "white noise". These three letters, therefore, generate all the other sounds.

There is a time-honored Kabbalistic meditation that derives from the *Sefer Yetzirah* ("Book of Creation"). This meditation is one of many based on the effects of sound, chanting, and breathing, as well as on the Hebrew letters, to elevate consciousness. Importantly, this particular form of meditation allows us to enter an altered state of awareness in a deliberate manner.

As we said, the three Hebrew letters of this intriguing

meditation are *Shin/Mem/Aleph*. The *Shin* makes the "Shhhh" sound. The *Mem* makes an "Mmmmm" sound. The *Aleph* is silent.

How does this meditation work? We know what white light is. It is composed of all the other colors; if we take all the colors and blend them together, we get white light. Now, the "Shhhh" sound of the *Shin* is an auditory version of white light called white noise. White noise is an amalgam of all the other frequencies. If we run various sounds through an oscilloscope —like a television screen—we will see that the "Shhhh" sound produces a chaotic pattern. On the same oscilliscope, the "Mmmmm" sound produces a very even wave: its height on top is equal to the height on the bottom, and it is symmetrically shaped.

Essentially, these two sounds relate to states of human consciousness. It is possible to use these to affect or alter our ordinary state of awareness. When these sounds are chanted over and over again, they have a mantra-like effect on us.

The Kabbalistic meditation, therefore, is to make use of these two sounds to achieve a specific state of consciousness. Unlike some forms of Eastern meditation, the Kabbalistic goal is not for us to experience passively our thoughts or the outer world; rather, it is for us to enter a definite sacred region within.

This meditation goes as follows: start with the *Shin* sound, then go to the *Mem* sound—this being a much higher inward state (corresponding to the *Sefira* of *Chokhmah* or wisdom)— and then return to the *Shin* sound. In other words, the chant goes back and forth, back and forth, like a swing. Go in and go out.

It is hard to remain in the *Mem* state for more than a few seconds, but gradually your excursion into it can be increased so that it encompasses a longer and longer period of time.

Simply sit comfortably. Begin by making the sound "Shhhh". Then switch to the "Mmmmm" sound. You are going to go back and forth. As you make the sound your body will vibrate in tune with a particular frequency, like a tuning fork.

After a while, you may find that the *Mem* sound will bring you into a new inner realm. Just allow yourself to linger there and then return with the *Shin* sound.

Initially, one minute for this meditative exercise is sufficient. Eventually, though, you may build up to five minutes. Since the *Mem* sound is connected to the divine realm of *Chokmah*, you can reach the state of *Chokmah* through this meditation.

When you perform this exercise, just experience the sound. Do not seek to utilize the sound for any purpose. Also, be sure to alternate between the "Shhhh" and the "Mmmmm" sounds. In this way, you remain in control of the experience.

The objective is to make the sound vibrate throughout your body. Just be one with the sound. Do not think about it or expect anything. Just be with the sound.

You can also perform this meditation silently. Simply make the sounds internally. Then your breathing pattern will be very different. If you perform the exercise aloud, then of course you must physically inhale and exhale.

Keeping in mind our meditation involving the *Shin/Mem*, let us go back to the first sentence of the Bible: "In the beginning, God created the heaven and the earth." In Hebrew, earth is *ha-aretz*, which comprises two parts: *ha* meaning "the" and *aretz* meaning "earth". Now, *aretz* is comprised of two parts: the *aleph* and the *ratz*. *Aretz* means "to run" and *aleph* is the letter *aleph*. Thus, *aretz* is "the running *aleph*".

From the viewpoint therefore of our previous meditation, we have here an instruction in the Bible's first sentence as to how to accomplish it. In the previous word, two "mother" letters exist; and then, the third "mother" letter is found. This passage intimates, then, that the *aleph* or silence should intervene—run back and forth—between the *Shin* and the *Mem*.

Kabbalistically, this sentence suggests that we should swing into the altered state of consciousness and then swing out of it. We go back in and out; we do not "stay" there. The way to build up our inner strength is to merely touch it and go out, to go and come back—and this is the concept of "running back and forth". In several accounts of the Prophets, like Ezekiel's, there is mention of something "running back and forth". Such allusions are always preparation for what is to occur after the meditation itself.

EXERCISE 2.   SHALOM MEDITATION

There is a very well-known Hebrew word that contains all this information: Shalom. It incorporates the "Shhhh" and the "Ommmm". Interestingly, then, the fundamental "Om" sound is found within this ancient Hebrew word meaning peace and wholeness, among its other connotations.

In chanting or orally meditating upon this word, we once more begin with the "Shhhh" sound and then blend into the "Mmmmm" sound. Kabbalists teach that you must not enter into the "Mmmmm" level immediately but just touch it and then come back to it. We can adjust to our own preferences the length of the "Shhhh" and the "Mmmmm" sounds. They do not have to be of equal length: we may prefer to dwell on each for varying durations.

As said in the previous meditation, this exercise goes all the way back to the Book of Ezekiel, wherein there is an allusion to a "running back and forth". Historically, Kabbalists have viewed this phrase as referring to methods of meditation such as this.

EXERCISE 3.   THE DAYS OF CREATION

One way to understand the essence of the *Sefiroth* is to keep in mind that the seven days of Creation involved the lowest seven of them. Each *Sefirah* contributed primarily to one particular day of Creation. If we therefore look at what was created on that day, we will have in one way a reflection of that *Sefirah*.

As we begin to contemplate that which was created on each day, we will gain insight into the nature of the respective *Sefirah*. For example, the *Sefirah* of the first day is *Chesed*. In this manner, we can use Chapter 1 of Genesis as a meditation.

A related technique is to use the verses pertaining to each day as a *mantra*. We just say those verses over and over again. Through this oral method, we can draw closer to discerning the essence of the ten *Sefiroth*.

EXERCISE 4. THE TREE OF LIFE

Let us now look at the famous diagram of the Tree of Life. In this particular diagram, the round circles are the ten *Sefiroth*. They are aligned in a certain way, one of many means to align them. Traditionally, though, this diagram depicts the most common alignment of the *Sefiroth*.

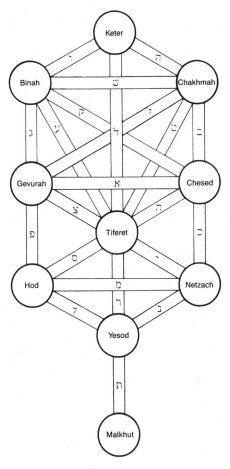

THE THIRTY-TWO PATHS

Notice that there are lines connecting the ten circles of the *Sefiroth*. If we connect the circles with the lines in this way, then there are exactly twenty-two lines. Is it a coincidence that there are precisely twenty-two letters in the Hebrew alphabet? We can see that there is a Hebrew letter for each line. These twenty-two lines and ten circles constitute the thirty-two possible paths toward the divine. Here we have encoded the major secrets of the universe. We can therefore use the diagram in a variety of ways. For example, we can construct a three-dimensional mandala of this and utilize it for visual meditation. This is a very powerful method. The central column is known as the Tree of Knowledge. It was forbidden to Adam only temporarily and is available to us through meditation. If Adam had waited until he had experienced the Sabbath, then it would have been permissible for him to eat of the Tree of Knowledge. Adam acted prematurely, but we have access to this structure through meditation.

EXERCISE 5-8. THE HEBREW LETTERS

We begin by selecting a Hebrew letter. Remember, each letter has three characteristics: a particular shape, a particular sound, and a numerical value, a corresponding number. The Kabbalah has for millennia taught that there are thirty-two secret paths of wisdom. The number thirty-two comes from the twenty-two letters and the ten *Sefiroth*.

Therefore, choose a Hebrew letter—for example, an *Aleph* —and start with its visual shape. Gaze at the letter until it is fixed in your visual field. Then close your eyes and continue to picture it. Bear in mind the Kabbalistic principle that each letter is really a mystical symbol. This is a simple meditation you can do with each of the letters.

A more advanced meditation is next to engrave the letter in your mind's eye. This would be as though you were chiseling the letter in stone.

The next step is to sculpt the letter. In doing so, you take away everything else. That is, when you chisel the letter, you

THE ALPHABET OF CREATION

א	ALEPH	1	ס	SAMECH	60
ב	BETH	2	ע	AYIN	70
ב	VETH	2	פ	PAY	80
ג	GIMEL	3	פ	PHAY	80
ד	DALETH	4	צ	TZADDE	90
ה	HAY	5	ק	KUPH	100
ו	VAV	6	ר	RESH	200
ז	ZAYIN	7	ש	SHIN	300
ח	CHETH	8	ש	SIN	300
ט	TETH	9	ת	TAV	400
י	YOD	10	ת	THAV	400
כ	CAPH	20	ך	FINAL CHAPH	500
כ	CHAPH	20	ם	FINAL MEM	600
ל	LAMED	30	ן	FINAL NUN	700
מ	MEM	40	ף	FINAL PHAY	800
נ	NUN	50	ץ	FINAL TZADDE	900

have the letter and also its background. With sculpting, though, you remove everything around the letter until only it remains—in relief. This is a very high-level meditative technique, for you have eliminated all the internal noise of thoughts —the "Shhhh"—and just the letter is left.

A still more advanced meditation is next to visualize the letter with your mind's eye as black fire. See the letter as a mystical symbol in black fire, on a background of white fire.

These are four different methods of meditation based on the Hebrew alphabet. Once we have done them with each individual letter, we can perform these spiritual exercises with two letters, and then perhaps even certain key words. On one level, these meditations help us to develop our power of visualization. But Kabbalists, of course, see more to these techniques than mere psychological practice. Rather, they have long regarded the Hebrew letters as possessing intrinsic meaning. From this perspective, meditation upon the Hebrew letters benefits us far more than a similar meditation based on the letters of the Roman alphabet.

This set of meditations is set forth in the *Sefer Yetzirah* ("Book of Creation"), the oldest known work on the Kabbalah. Tradition has it that its author was Abraham.

Interestingly, Kabbalists teach that Abraham was the progenitor of many other mystical systems besides the Jewish. Their reference point is the line in Genesis that recounts: "Abraham blessed his other children besides Isaac, gave them gifts, and sent them to the East." Many people have concurred with this ancient statement. For instance, some modern-day Indian gurus trace their own tradition back to Abraham because of this biblical verse. For Abraham had many children besides Isaac and the gifts he gave them—all the commentaries agree—were not material, but gifts of spiritual teachings. They took them to the East and thereby established the foundation of the Eastern esoteric systems. For this reason we can certainly expect to find many similarities between the Kabbalah—as transmitted through Abraham—and the Eastern mystical paths.

EXERCISE 9.   THE CIRCLE OF LETTERS

There is an intriguing Kabbalistic meditation described historically as a prerequisite for creating material forms such as *Golems*. This meditation derives from the Book of Formation, which appeared in written form between the third and sixth centuries C.E.

Imagine yourself in the center of a circle. The circle consists of the letters of the Hebrew alphabet; the twenty-two letters surround you. Imagine each letter as a three-dimensional figure like a sculpture standing before you. View each figure as though you possess panascopic vision, being able to see behind you as well as in front of you, so that you are actually seeing 360 degrees. You can see the letters behind you and before you simultaneously.

When you are able to visualize this, make a connection between the first letter and the second letter. Then make a connection between the first letter and third letter, and so forth, until you have made all the connections. According to Kabbalists, each of these links represents a manifestation of divine energy.

Now you have not only visualized each of the Hebrew letters clearly in front of you—and have visualized all of them simultaneously—but you have made a connection between every other letter. When you have done this, you have actually created a mandala. And this can be used as a visual meditative device.

If you wish, you can construct this mandala and practice meditating upon it. Or, you can simply meditate upon the image in your mind's eye.

A more advanced method of the "Hebrew mandala" meditation is to place only the three "mother" letters around the circle, instead of all the letters.

APPENDIX 1

1. Two things that are similar are the same.
There is no space, no division, in the spiritual realm. Space is in the physical plane, where two similar things are ultimately different. But on the spiritual plane, similar things are the same. Example: similar angels are the same. Thus, on one level—the spiritual one—all people are the same.
On the physical plane, physical barriers are required to separate similar things from one another. Example: all of the water in an ocean is one; however, a glass is needed to separate some of the water.

2. Things that are different cannot meet, join or link.

3. Spiritual distance is measured by similarity and difference.
Example: Distance from God is measured by how similar one is to God's prescribed life for man.

4. Nothing can be destroyed on the spiritual plane.
Once something exists on the spiritual plane, it will always exist. Spiritual things exist forever. All things exist by God's will. That divine will is perfect, continuous, eternal. God's memory is perfect. Therefore, once thought of by God, an object is not forgotten. All things in the universe exist in God's mind. Consequently, all things are eternal.

5. Spiritual matters are dependent on physical aspects to allow them to be distinguished, to exist as separate entities.
Therefore, all spiritual forces are dependent on the physical universe. Which came first? They are interdependent. The *Sefiroth* are intermediaries. The planes are physical, spiritual, and—the highest—beyond.

6. The *Ain Sof* is not bound by rules of logic; it is as different from the spiritual as it is from the physical. God is beyond all classification and planes.

APPENDIX 2

THE BIBLICAL ACCOUNT OF CREATION AND EVOLUTION

1. There is a significant difference between Chapters 1 and 2 in Genesis. Chapter 1 concerns creation as told by *Elohim* (Justice). Chapter 2 is creation as told by a different name or attribute of God, *Adonai Elohim* (Mercy). The latter also involves a different *Sefira*.

2. Chapter 2:4 ends with "earth" before "heaven", in reverse order from Chapter 1. Also, the word "completed" is used instead of "made". One explanation of the difference is that Chapter 1 is actually a planning stage, a thought process, and Chapter 2 describes what actually happens, an action process.

3. Another Kabbalistic explanation is that Chapter 1 is a spiritual description, an overview. The *Sephira* conceptualized the "big picture", whereas the physical account in Chapter 2 is a detailed description.

4. There are fifteen billion years between Chapters 1 and 2. Verse 2:4 starts with *Aiy leh*. Where else in the Bible does this phrase appear? Jewish mystics point out that *aiy leh* always denotes whenever something new appears in the Bible. Thus, Chapter 1 is one event. Chapter 2 is a different event. "This is (*aiy leh*) a totally new story we are going to tell." The fifteen billion year time difference accounts for evolution. Kabbalistically, this explanation was put into writing about six hundred years ago.

5. The Sabbath Day is described at the beginning of Chapter 2. The Sabbath therefore indicates the separating and linking—the barrier/border—between Chapters 1 and 2.

6. The actual Hebrew words of the Bible give a clue as to intent. The first universe is called *Bereah*, which means "created". It is an archetypal idea. The second universe is indicated by the words *Vayahe Chain Yetzirah*, or "formation" of things. The third universe is suggested by the use of the word *Asiyah*, "made" or "completed" in physical terms. It indicates that a final adjustment is being made, possibly a final mutation to meet the plan; God "fine-tunes".

The progression goes as follows: Creation, Evolution, Adjustment.

APPENDIX 3

SOME NOTES ON GENESIS

1. In Genesis 1:4, the words "heaven" and "earth" are followed by "earth/heaven". There is a debate as to whether the spiritual or the physical came first. The Kabbalistic concept is that without the physical, the spiritual could not exist. Spirituality and its growth occur in a physical body.

2. Chapter 1 relates that God said, "Let us make man in our image." Chapter 2 relates, "God formed man out of dust of the ground." In Eden, "He placed the man that he had formed." This man is Adam, *not* the creation mentioned in Chapter 1 fifteen billion years before.

3. Kabbalists teach that God allowed for a certain period of evolution to take place, for man to evolve to a certain point. Six thousand years ago, Adam was to play a key role in the Messianic plan. God's original design was for the evolved man, Adam, to be the Messiah. This giant step reflects that Adam was at a point of evolution, capability, and potential for tremendous spiritual unfoldment. That same potential exists now for each of us. Adam was a new, different species; he did not come through the regular, evolutionary chain of events.

That is, Adam was formed and placed in the Garden of Eden, a higher plane of existence. He was to be the teacher showing the spiritual route. But something went wrong—this we clearly know. There are clues in the account about Cain that there were many people outside the Garden of Eden. For instance, Cain pleads to God, "They will find me and kill me." We are likewise informed, "And Cain knew his wife. . ." and "He was building a city." All such references indicate that there were many people around at this time.

4.   In Chapter 1, the children of *Elohim* (God) were the created ones. In Chapter 2, fifteen billion years later, the sons of God married the daughters of Adam (humanity), the latter a new and different species. Ezekiel is an example of a son of Adam.

5.   Adam, the formed man, was different from created, evolved man in the following respects:
    a.   Adam had longevity—he lived about 1,000 years.
    b.   Adam had the power of prophecy—he talked to God. A prophet is one who can channel spiritual energy, who speaks with God.
    c.   Adam had a soul.
    d.   Adam had no foreskin.
    e.   Adam had no attachment to good or evil.
    Through intermarriage between Adam's species and the other humans, these qualities would become diluted. Longevity and prophecy were altered—diminished—through successive generations.

6.   We count time in this cycle from Adam's creation. Things "go wrong" because of the need for free will to exist. The only way to have free will is through evil. Evil splits us off from good (God). The task for each of us is to return to the good.

APPENDIX 4

THE NATURE OF THE HUMAN SOUL

Kabbalists teach that every living thing has a soul. There is a vegetable soul. There is also an animal soul, which has feelings, intelligence, imagination, and memory. Divine soul binds us to the highest spiritual levels. Each human has all three souls.

The divine soul has five components: *Nefesh*, *Ruach*, *Neshamah*, *Chayyah*, and *Yechidah*. In this realm, we have access to the first three of these. Each of the five components relates to one of five universes and five *partzufim*.

The traditional Kabbalistic analogy is to the glass blower: *Nefesh* is where the breath of the blower rests; it is most removed from the glassmaker and is the object being blown. *Ruach* is breath in motion. *Neshamah* is the breath of the blower/maker. *Chayyah* is the air in the glass blower's lungs, his life-force. *Yechidah* is the psyche of the blower, his will, his desire to blow the glass.

Nefesh means "to rest". God gave the soul to the world on the seventh day, the Sabbath.

We can experience the soul through meditation, by putting the body in a state of rest. *Ruach* means "wind" or air-in-motion. We feel the soul-in-motion, the movement of the Holy Spirit within us. *Neshamah* means "to breathe". This refers to an inspired state, a sense of the soul's origins. We feel our breath. *Chayyah* is "life" or "living". This was Adam's level. *Yechidah* means "oneness", merging with the divine.

A note: the English word "intimate" indicates closeness through feeling the other's breath.

Ain Sof means "no thing". The letters in *Ain* can be arranged to spell *ani*, which means "I". The real me is that part of me that is part of God. We say, "my book" or "my body", "my mind" or "my soul". The real me is the part of *Ain Sof* within me, the divine spark.

APPENDIX 5

DREAMS AND THE KABBALAH

Jewish mystics teach that the divine soul separates from the physical body during sleep. *Nefesh*, the animal soul, remains attached to the body. The divine soul is attached to the animal soul, which connects to the physical body. Once separated from the physical body, the divine soul can have meetings and informational experiences on higher planes of existence. If information is communicated to the body, then it travels through the levels of the soul—through *nefesh*—to the animal soul.

The higher souls are free to leave the body and do whatever spiritual beings, at their respective levels, can do. *Nefesh* may wish to transmit information to the person's consciousness. It would proceed from *neshamah* to *ruach* to *nefesh* to animal soul, resulting in its stimulation by means of an image. Dreams can come from the physical body by stimulating the animal soul through physical stimulation. Thus, dreaming is seen as a function of the animal soul and related to imagination.

Dreams can also come from the divine soul, but they must pass through the animal soul. We see an image of the heavenly message, but it must be decoded. In any given dream, all three levels can be operative. We must be attentive to the source of the dream and its type of message.

Prophets' dreams give a clearer message, not as clouded by the physical and the animal soul. Prophets' dreams receive information in a clearer manner, without clutter. They are therefore more "pure" dreams than those of ordinary men and women.

GLOSSARY

Adam Kadmon. The fifth or highest universe. It provides the "blueprint" for the lower four, of which ours is at the bottom.

Ain Sof. God or the "Infinite", from which all forms in the universe are created. Kabbalists teach that *Ain Sof* created the Ten *Sefiroth* as a link from man to Him.

Ain Sof Ohr. The "Infinite Light", the primary emanation of *Ain Sof.*

Asiyah. The universe of "action", the lowest of the four below *Adam Kadmon.* This is our cosmos, where deeds are paramount.

Atziluth. The universe of "emanation". It is the highest dominion of existence and encompasses the pure dimension of the primary "forces" of the divine, the *Sefiroth.*

Baal Shem Tov. "Bearer of the Good Name", the popular appellation of Israel ben Eliezer (c. 1698-1760), the charismatic founder of *Hasidism.*

Beriyah. The universe of "creation", the second highest below *Adam Kadmon.* The evanescent archetypes of the first universe are organized here into a coherent order.

Betulah. A virgin.

Binah. One of the Ten *Sefiroth*, usually translated as "understanding".

Bohu. Literally, "he is there". In Kabbalistic metaphysics, this state preceded the existence of our universe and was associated with *tohu.*

Chayah. One of the highest manifestations of the human soul; it becomes operative in the afterlife.

Cherubim. Two angel-like figurines that were situated above the holy ark in the Temple of Jerusalem. Divine prophecy was said to be transmitted between them.

Chesed. One of the Ten *Sefiroth*, usually translated as "mercy".

Chokmah. One of the Ten *Sefiroth*, usually translated as "wisdom".

Daath. An intermediary force, usually translated as "knowledge", between the *Sefirotic* triad of *Keter, Hokmah,* and *Binah*.

Eleh. Literally, "And then". Each time this word appears in the Bible, it signifies that a new level of the narrative has begun.

Elokim. One of the Ten Names of God mentioned in the Bible. Also, an abbreviation for the five *partzufim*.

Et. A biblical word, Kabbalistically interpreted to signify the cosmic forces of Creation represented by the letters of the Hebrew alphabet.

Etz Pri. Literally, tree-fruit or a tree that is fruit. According to Kabbalists, God intended a fruit-tree to be created on the third day, but nature instead produced a tree that bore fruit.

Gaon. A great scholar or genius.

Gevurah. One of the Ten *Sefiroth*, usually translated as "judgment".

Gilgul, gilgulim (plural). The "cycles" or "transformations" of each soul's journey to complete enlightenment. This concept assumes the existence of reincarnation and many lifetimes on earth for each person.

Golem. A legendary being of clay, created through Kabbalistic ritual. Reference to *Golems* can be found as early as in the Talmud.

Hasidism. The popular, charismatic movement which arose among East European Jewry in the late eighteenth century. *Hasid* means "pious" in Hebrew; in twelfth-century Germany, an unrelated group was likewise known as the *Hasidim*.

Hod. One of the Ten *Sefiroth*, usually translated as "glory".

Kabbalah. From the Hebrew root-word "to receive". Often used as a generic term for Jewish mysticism per se, it more precisely refers to its esoteric thought from the late twelfth century onward.

Malkuth. The "kingdom" or lowest of the Ten *Sefiroth*; it is also regarded as the passive, receptive force in the cosmos. See also *kether.*

Mantra. A Sanskrit term for a meditational sound, such as a word or phrase, chanted or said inwardly to effect higher consciousness.

Mayim. "Water"—or, more esoterically, the fundamental substance that preceded matter in the creation of the universe.

Mezuzah (pl. *mezzuzoth*). Literally, "doorpost". A small case containing a piece of parchment upon which is written the prayer that begins *Shema Yisrael.* This case is affixed to each right doorpost in a Jew's home, in accordance with the biblical injunction.

Midrash. The legendary tradition of Judaism. A *midrash* (in lower case, with the plural *midrashim*) is a specific Midrashic legend.

Mikveh. The ritual bath.

Mitzvah (pl. *mitzvoth*). A divine commandment or "binding point" to God; a good deed. There are 613 *mitzvoth* specified in the Bible, many of which pertain to rituals involved with the Temple of Jerusalem.

Moshiach. Literally, "the anointed one" or "the one to be appointed", referring to the Messiah. He is prophecied in the Bible to descend from the House of David. Kabbalists intimate that in every generation there is one such individual who can be the *Moshiach* if the world has sufficiently redeemed itself.

Na'areh. A young girl.

Nachash. The creature—often translated as "serpent"—who seduced Eve into eating from the forbidden Tree of Knowledge.

Nefesh. The lowest, most physical portion of the human Self. The *nefesh* dissolves upon physical mortality.

Neshamah. The nonphysical, transcendent part of the Self. The *neshamah* continues after bodily death; below *chayah* and *yechidah* in the hierarchy within the soul.

Noahide Laws. The seven divine laws incumbent on all humanity to obey, communicated by God to Noah after the Flood.

Partzuf (pl. *partzufim*). The Kabbalah teaches that the Ten *Sefiroth* became reconstituted as five *partzufim* when the divine "breaking of the vessels" took place.

Rakiah. Sky or barrier; interface.

Ruach. That portion of the human Self that is intermediate in nature between the *nefesh* and *neshamah.* The *ruach* dissipates shortly after bodily death.

Satan. In Judaism, a very loyal servant of God who enables human free will to exist through offering the option of evil.

Sefer Gilgulim. The "Book of Cycles", written by Rabbi Chaim Vital, a disciple of Rabbi Isaac Luria in sixteenth-century Safed in Israel. This treatise deals extensively with the subject of reincarnation.

Sefer Yetzirah. "Book of Creation", anonymously written between the third and sixth centuries C.E. It represents the earliest metaphysical text in the Hebrew language.

Sefiroth (also written as Sephirot). The ten energy essences that are said to be in constant interplay and underlie all of the universe. The *Sefiroth* have historically been portrayed in various arrangements, the most significant being the Tree of Life.

Septuagint. The Greek translation of the Bible.

Shedim. Demons or potentially destructive forces said to exist in the spiritual realm.

Tallis. A four-cornered prayer shawl with fringes at the corners, worn by men during various prayer services.

Tefillin. Phylacteries worn at the morning services (except Sabbath) by men and boys over the age of thirteen.

Teshuvah. Repentance, or more broadly, return and ascent to one's divine source of origin. *Teshuvah* is said to have existed before the Creation of our universe.

Tetragrammaton. The four-letter Ineffable Name of God: YHVH. It comprises the letters *Yud/Hey/Vov/Hey.* Its true pronunciation is believed to have been lost, and the knowledge of it is believed to confer great power.

Tifereth. One of the Ten *Sefiroth,* usually translated as "beauty".

Tikkuney Zohar. "Emmendations to the *Zohar*", written a few years after the *Zohar,* around the year 1300.

Tohu. Confusion, chaos.

Torah. In a narrow sense, the Pentateuch. More widely, Torah is understood to comprise the twenty-four books of the Bible and the Talmud.

Tree of Life. The central metaphor for the universe and every aspect of it. The Ten *Sefiroth* are most typically arranged in a pattern known as the Tree of Life; all animate and inanimate forms are said to mirror this structure.

Yesod. One of the Ten *Sefiroth,* usually translated as "foundation".

Yetzirah. One of the four universes below *Adam Kadmon,* that of "formation". Here the potentialities built up in the higher two are activated.

Yom Kippur. The Day of Atonement, the most holy day of the Jewish year, spent in fasting and prayer. It is regarded as the Day of Judgment, on which God decides whether or not a person will be inscribed in the Book of Life for the coming year.

Zohar. The "Book of Splendor", which first appeared in late thirteenth-century Spain. It is the "bible" of the Kabbalah and its most influential work. Ascribed to Simeon bar Yochai of the second century by traditionalists, scholars today attribute it to Moses de Leon, who is said to have composed most of it in the 1280s and 1290s. See *Tikkuney Zohar.*

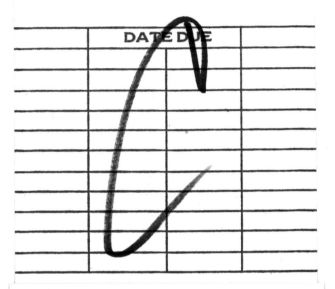